WINDOWS ON **WORLD WAR II**

A collection of iconic events from the second global conflict

WINDOWS ON WORLD WAR II

A collection of iconic events from the second global conflict

EDWARD KIESTER JR

Contents

Introduction

The Great War of 1914–18 was billed at 'The War to End All Wars'. But it was far from that. Within a generation, the same combatants were at it again, albeit with minor adjustments in their alliances. Italy and Japan, which had been on the Allied side in World War I, joined Germany in the Berlin–Rome–Tokyo 'Axis'. The 'Allies' were, again, Britain, France and Russia (by then renamed the Soviet Union), plus, from late 1941, the United States. Chian, neutral in World War I, backed the Allies in World War II. Smaller countries lined up on both sides.

World War II was truly a global conflict. More than one hundred million soldiers from sixty-one countries were involved, and armed forces struggled everywhere, from Asia's tropical jungles and the Saharan sands to the windswept steppes of the Soviet Union and the snowfields of the high Arctic. Mechanised warfare, in its infancy in World War I, played a key role, resulting in much greater death tolls, especially among civilians. More than sixty million people were to die in World War II, of whom more than half were non-combatants.

Germany's invasion of Poland on 1 September 1939 is traditionally considered the start of World War II. But countries had been fighting for almost a decade before that—in China, East Africa and Spain, among other places. Indeed, one viewpoint says that World War I never ended, and World War II was simply another chapter in the same bloody struggle.

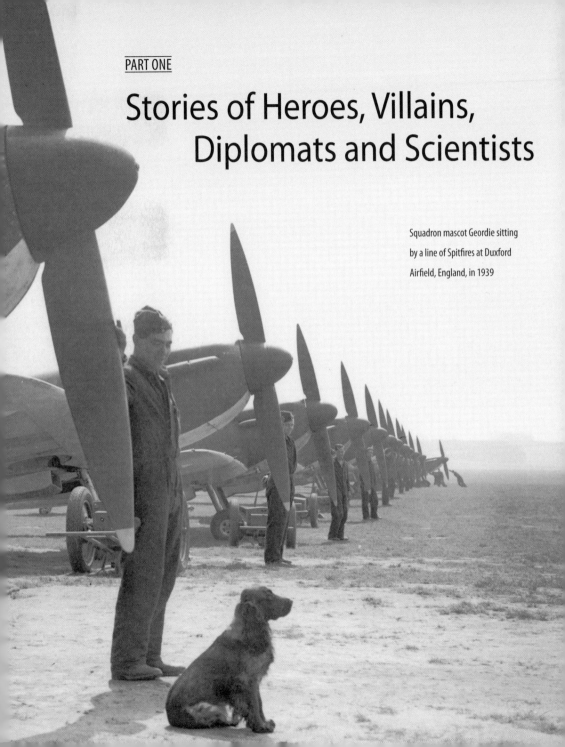

PART ONE

Stories of Heroes, Villains, Diplomats and Scientists

Squadron mascot Geordie sitting
by a line of Spitfires at Duxford
Airfield, England, in 1939

'Peace In Our Time'—Not

Neville Chamberlain and the Munich Crisis

On the night of 3 September 1939, with the ink barely dry on the Allied declarations of war, ten Royal Air Force planes flew over the industrial cities of Germany's Ruhr, activating air-raid alarms. The twin-engined aircraft were Bristol Blenheims, classed as light bombers, with a 2,250-kilometre range and capable of carrying a half-tonne of bombs. But the payload that night was neither incendiaries nor explosives. Rather, the planes dropped what were referred to as 'white bombs', containing six million leaflets. These warned the residents of the Ruhr, 'Your rulers have condemned you to the massacres, miseries and privations of a war they cannot ever hope to win'.

Two days later, the Blenheims were back, this time over the cities of Hamburg, Bremen, Kiel and Cologne. New leaflets told the residents of those cities that, while they existed on war rations, their leaders were carrying vast sums of money abroad. Heinrich Himmler, the leaflets declared, had already taken out more than a half million marks. Before the war was a month old, thirty-one million leaflets had been dropped. By the end of 1939, the total would be more than a hundred million.

The 'bombphlets' were the first 'shots' of what British newspapers and critics derisively labelled the 'Confetti War'. An early joke told how one pilot had been reprimanded when he inadvertently dropped leaflets still bound together in a brick-like package. 'Good God! You might have killed someone!' he was supposedly told.

Prime Minister Chamberlain displaying the 'peace accord' signed with Hitler in September 1938

The paper bombardment also opened an early phase of what would become known as the Phoney War, during which ostensible enemies France and Germany faced each other across their borders without exchanging gunfire, a peaceable interlude that went on for the next six months. Winston Churchill termed it 'The Twilight War'. Germans called it the sitzkrieg, or 'sitting war', punning on blitzkrieg. Not to be outpunned, the British dubbed it 'The Bore War', a play on 'Boer War'.

Despite the derision, the Confetti War was a serious, last-ditch attempt to avert all-out war. It was authorised by the British prime minister, Neville Chamberlain, holding, in the face of scepticism, to his belief that men of reason could be counted on to reach a sensible settlement of a dispute if they would only sit down and discuss it. At the time, and for decades after, Chamberlain was caricatured as a befuddled negotiator who clung to his trademark furled umbrella—a symbol for many of his caution and timorousness—while steadily giving ground to Britain's enemies. In the eyes of his detractors, he reached his nadir during the September 1938 negotiations with Adolf Hitler in Munich, where he yielded to numerous demands from the dictator before returning home waving an agreement that he said achieved 'peace with honour'. He proclaimed, 'I am a man of peace to the depths of my soul', but as the agreement unravelled, Chamberlain's policy quickly came to be seen as symptomatic of cowardice. Only later in the twentieth century was it acknowledged that the policy might have been justified, and that Chamberlain's actions delayed war and gained the Allies valuable time.

A TRUE ENGLISH GENTLEMAN

Neville Chamberlain was the quintessential English gentleman, right down (or up) to his wing collar and bowler hat. The son of one noted prime minister and half-brother of another, he at first eschewed politics in favour of a career in the colonies. After five unsuccessful years trying to establish a sisal plantation in the Bahamas, he returned home and soon became mayor of Birmingham. He served briefly in Lloyd George's Liberal government before switching to the Conservative Party, for which he was elected to Parliament in 1918. He held several lower-level posts in Conservative governments, and in 1931 was named Chancellor of the Exchequer. In 1937, he succeeded Stanley Baldwin as prime minister.

As Chancellor, Chamberlain had set the nation's economic policy. Like most countries, Britain had suffered severely in the Depression; attempting to balance the budget, the Baldwin government cut funds for the military and for armaments. As prime minister, Chamberlain authorised some rearmament, while claiming, 'The country is strong. She is getting stronger every day'. Warned by fellow Conservative Winston Churchill about

THE UNINVITED ENVOY

In the early phase of World War II, attempts to make peace deals were made by many parties, with diplomatic overtures coming from some unexpected quarters. On 10 May 1941, farmer David McLean was walking across Floors Farm near Eaglesham, Scotland, when he spied a man trying to extricate himself from a parachute harness. 'Good evening', the man said in stilted English. 'I am Alfred Horn of the German Air Force. I wish to see the Duke of Hamilton. Please take me to him immediately.' It was soon established, however, that the man was not Alfred Horn but Rudolf Hess, Hitler's deputy, and that he

had flown to Scotland on one of the most mysterious missions of the war.

Hess wanted the Duke of Hamilton to persuade Winston Churchill to negotiate peace terms with Hitler, so that the two countries could unite to fight against the Bolsheviks. But to Hess's dismay, the British government refused. After being detained until the end of the conflict, Hess was tried as a war criminal and spent the rest of his life in Berlin's Spandau Prison. Hearing of Hess's capture, Hitler declared him insane. Whether Hitler had sent Hess on a mission or known of his flight is still hotly debated.

a rearming Germany, Chamberlain stepped up development of combat aircraft like the fabled Spitfires and Hurricanes that were to play a key role in the Battle of Britain, but saw no point in heavily rearming 'for a war that might never come'.

Chamberlain was energetic, a workaholic who spent hours at his desk; supporters saw his devotion to duty and hands-on, personal diplomacy as evidence of strength. Even admirers, though, admitted he could be arrogant, snobbish, ill-at-ease with strangers, a stumbling speaker and certainly not a classic political glad-hander. Chamberlain himself acknowledged, after watching newsreel footage of himself, that he appeared pompous and wooden. His major characteristic was doggedness: once he had taken a position, he refused to back down, compromise, accept advice or admit error; when he was sharply criticised or attacked, one colleague said, 'His hand went to his sword'.

He kept his own counsel, confiding his opinions and inner thoughts only to his sister Hilda, in lengthy letters. After a dispute with his foreign secretary, Anthony Eden, Chamberlain made foreign affairs his personal fief, despite his lack of experience. Before his first controversial trip to meet 'Herr Hitler', he consulted merely four people, only two of whom were in the government.

Chamberlain believed that any problem could be solved by men of goodwill. Thus, when Hitler began eyeing up the Sudetenland border region of Czechoslovakia, Chamberlain was sure the situation could be resolved amicably. 'If we can bring these nations into friendly discussion, into settling of their differences, we will have saved the peace of Europe for a generation', he said. Then he set off ('hat in hand', detractors were to say) to visit Hitler in his redoubt at Berchtesgaden in the Bavarian Alps.

Czechoslovakia in 1938 had the strongest army in Europe, made up of forty divisions. Its famous Skoda armaments works provided Czechoslovakia and many other European countries

> Chamberlain believed that any problem could be solved by men of goodwill. Thus, when Hitler began eyeing up the Sudetenland ... Chamberlain was sure the situation could be resolved amicably.

with weapons, and these factories lay close to the German border. Surrender of the mountainous Sudetenland would not only rob the nation of a natural defensive barrier but also bring the Skoda works within range of German guns. Nonetheless, Chamberlain 'agreed in principle' to Hitler's proposed takeover, since that would presumably guarantee peace. In return, Hitler accepted that an international commission would draw up the new frontiers. Feeling abandoned by nominal ally Britain, President Edvard Benes of Czechoslovakia went along with the plan, even though the loss of the Sudetenland would leave his country defenceless, and rob it of much of its industrial base, as well as eight hundred thousand non-Germanic Czech citizens.

'PEACE IN OUR TIME'

Chamberlain had no sooner come home to London to proclaim 'peace in our time' than Hitler changed his mind and upped the terms. He dismissed the idea of an international commission; he wanted possession of the Sudetenland—immediately. Chamberlain dutifully trooped off to Munich on 28 September, where this time he was joined by the French premier, Edouard Daladier, and the Italian Duce, Benito Mussolini.

Daladier was for standing firm, but Chamberlain insisted on giving in to Hitler. It was not peace at any price, he said; Hitler had pledged that he would make no further demands. The world breathed a sigh of relief and acclaimed Chamberlain a peacemaker. Hitler thought otherwise. According to one English diplomat in Berlin, 'Hitler regarded the Prime Minister as an impertinent busybody who spoke the ridiculous jargon of an outmoded democracy'. Mussolini echoed this, telling his son-in-law and foreign minister, Count Galeazzo Ciano, 'These men are not made of the same stuff as the Francis Drakes and the other magnificent adventurers who created the British Empire. They are the tired sons of a long line of rich forefathers and they will lose their empire'.

On 3 October, to a startled House of Commons, Chamberlain displayed his signed agreement with Hitler and declared that the man he had formerly called 'utterly untrustworthy and dishonest' was 'a man who could be relied upon when he has given his word'. Though many members of the House, including some of the prime minister's supporters, were appalled that he seemed to be turning his back on Czechoslovakia, they gave him their grudging support. But the speech marked the beginning of the prime minister's long slide in public esteem. Czechoslovakia was divided into Bohemia–Moravia and Slovakia, and the following March German troops rolled into Prague and took over the entire country. A week later, Germany claimed the Baltic port of Memel, began menacing the German-speaking Free City of Danzig on the Polish border and threatened Poland itself. At Daladier's behest, Chamberlain joined France in declaring that if Hitler moved again against a smaller country, he must be stopped. On 31 March 1939, the two countries signed a declaration pledging to come to Poland's aid if it were attacked.

The attack came on 1 September 1939. Following the signing of the Nazi–Soviet Nonaggression Pact, German tanks rolled across the Polish border while the Soviets occupied eastern Poland. Still hopeful that a peaceable solution could be worked out, Chamberlain gave Berlin what he considered an ultimatum: if Hitler withdrew his troops within two days, Britain would host an international conference where the parties could negotiate. Hitler ignored the offer, and Parliament was aghast at Chamberlain. During a debate in the Commons on the evening of 2 September, an outraged Leo Amery, Chamberlain's longtime friend, staunch supporter and fellow Conservative, famously turned his back on the prime minister and cried across the House to Arthur

Greenwood, leader of the Opposition, 'Speak for England, Arthur!' The next day, the House voted for war on Germany, and a reluctant Chamberlain was forced to accept the decision.

THE PHONEY WAR

Hitler's blitzkrieg routed Poland in three weeks, with Britain and France unable to offer any help. There followed six months of the Phoney War, during which Chamberlain stepped up an industrious program of rearmament, with particular emphasis on building a protective Royal Air Force, and continued his leaflet campaign.

The expulsion of British troops from Norway following an ill-planned operation to oppose German invasion forces there in April 1940 turned many more members of Chamberlain's party

A British airman prepares a leaflet drop

against him. When Germany invaded Holland and Belgium in May, Parliament turned to Winston Churchill to head a government of national unity. Chamberlain remained in government as Lord President of the Council, confident he would later be returned to power. But with the fall of France in June, he would fade from the scene. In midsummer 1940, he developed stomach cancer and within six months of his downfall he was dead.

The condemnation of his appeasement policies did not die with him, however. In July 1940, a searing examination of the events leading up to the war, *Guilty Men*, by three leftist journalists using the pen name CATO, became an immediate bestseller. It vilified Chamberlain and his prime ministerial predecessors, Stanley Baldwin and Ramsey MacDonald, for their failure to take a stand against evil, and held them responsible for thousands and thousands of deaths. More attacks followed, including *Why England Slept*, by the future U.S. President John F. Kennedy, and Winston Churchill's multivolume memoirs. The Chamberlain-as-weakling thesis became firmly embedded, the stuff of gospel.

In the mid-1960s, however, the reasons for Chamberlain's policies were re-examined. First of all, it was noted that, at the time of Munich, Britain was only two decades removed from the horrors of World War I. The deaths of a million young men in the muddy trenches of France had left a deep scar on the national psyche, and no one was anxious to repeat that dreadful experience. Second, Britain had been seriously weakened by the 1930s Depression, as no one knew better than the former Chancellor of the Exchequer. The country could scarcely face the costs of rearmament and a major war. Moreover, it was said, Britain had narrowly escaped a proletarian uprising during the Depression. The upper-crust government, including Chamberlain, feared a new war might touch off a revolution, as it had in Bolshevik Russia twenty years before.

> The deaths of a million young men in the muddy trenches of France had left a deep scar on the national psyche, and no one was anxious to repeat that dreadful experience.

Militarily, the country was ill-equipped to match German might; the advanced planes and tanks that were to be so important in the 1940s fighting were not available in 1938. On the political front, Britain had lost two of its allies from World War I: Japan had become a direct threat to the British Empire in the Pacific, and Italy had become a full-fledged partner in Hitler's Axis. France was the only possible European ally, and it was shaky. America remained firmly committed, in 1938, to isolationism. The Soviet Union was unreliable and politically unacceptable. Czechoslovakia and Poland were not traditional allies or close neighbours. For all these reasons, the new reasoning went, the Munich agreement was justified. At the very least, it was said, Chamberlain's much criticised appeasement had bought Britain nearly two years of time to mobilise for the war 'the man of peace' could not envision and did not want.

The Secret Weapon That Won the Battle of Britain

Robert Watson-Watt and the Development of Radar

Mist shrouded the English Channel that Sunday morning, 15 September 1940, as German bombers lumbered across the sky—139 Heinkels and Dorniers, carrying heavy bomb loads earmarked for London. Above and below them and wingtip to wingtip, 679 single-seater Messerschmitt 109s and 110s, the largest number of fighters ever seen, flew a bristling escort, ready for a showdown. This was to be the Luftwaffe's coup de grace, a monster knockout punch that would obliterate the last elements of the RAF and give the Germans total control of the skies, in preparation for Hitler's vaunted 'Operation Sea Lion', a full-scale invasion of Britain. Bombers had been hammering British airfields, factories and cities for nearly a month. German boats were preparing to cross the Channel and storm the beaches.

But before the German planes even reached the English coast, another massive flock of planes loomed out of the mist. Royal Air Force Spitfires and Hurricanes pounced onto the Luftwaffe formation, dividing it in half, scattering the fighters and tattooing the bombers with machine-gun fire. Anti-aircraft batteries joined in. Soon parachutes and falling aircraft dotted the skies. The bombers rumbled on, but in such disarray that most missed their targets and were forced to jettison their bombs. Somehow, the RAF seemed to know, as if by telepathy, precisely when and in what numbers the Luftwaffe would arrive over British skies.

On 17 September, the last day on which tides, weather and daylight hours would favour an invasion before winter set in, the Germans tried again. But once more, the RAF was able to anticipate the arrival of the German aircraft. The Spitfires and Hurricanes intercepted and held off the German strike, shooting down nearly one hundred planes while losing only a handful of their own. At 11 am, the remaining attackers were forced to turn tail and head for home. Hitler then postponed Operation Sea Lion indefinitely, and the invasion plan was never revived.

'Their finest hour', Winston Churchill famously said of the undermanned and undergunned, mainly nineteen- and twenty-year-old RAF pilots who turned back the Luftwaffe again and again in the 'Battle of Britain' and frustrated Hitler's dream. 'Never

Luftwaffe bomb London during the Battle of Britain

in the field of human conflict have so many owed so much to so few.' But there was another hero of that victory, sitting on the other side of London, watching lines on an oscilloscope. He was a little-known, bespectacled, middle-aged Scottish civil servant and engineer, whose technological wizardry and organisational skills had had a huge impact not only on aerial combat and aviation generally but also on many other aspects of modern life. His name was Robert Watson-Watt, and he was the inventor of radar.

CLUES IN THE STORMS

Robert Watson-Watt was a descendant of the inventor of the steam engine, James Watt, and he had the same kind of curiosity as the ancestor who watched a boiling tea-kettle and wondered how to harness its energy. By twenty-first-century standards, Robert might be described as a nerd. Under 170 centimetres tall and weighing 84 kilograms, he self-deprecatingly declared that friends described him as 'chubby' while others more realistically said he was 'tubby'. Graduating in 1912 from the University of St Andrews near his home in Dundee, Scotland, with 'special distinction' in electrical engineering, he taught at the university for a year, then when World War I came, applied for a position in the War Office. The War Office said his educational credentials didn't fit their needs, but passed him off to the Meteorological Office.

It was a fortuitous change. Those were the pioneering days of radio, also known then as 'wireless telegraphy', and Watson-Watt, at university, had become fascinated by the physics of radio waves. He was posted to the Branch Meteorological Office at the Royal Aircraft Establishment and asked to investigate whether radio waves could be used to predict and locate thunderstorms, an obvious hazard to fliers. Watson-Watt was sure they could and, over the next years, devoted himself to the so-called 'Thunderstorm Enquiry'. By 1922, he had established that by transmitting short radio waves in the direction of a storm and then measuring the time it took for an echo, or 'bounce', to be detected, you could calculate not only the location of the storm, but also its direction and speed. Watson-Watt even managed to rig up an early cathode-ray tube (similar to a TV) so that an image of the source of the echo would appear on the screen.

Watson-Watt was not the only scientist investigating radio waves. As early as 1887, the German physicist Heinrich Hertz had experimented with radio waves and succeeded in both generating and detecting them. (A wave's frequency is measured in hertz, as a tribute to him.) The Dutch scientist Christian Huelsmeyer had used radio echoes to detect ships' locations and thus avert collisions. In 1922, two scientists from the U.S. Naval Research

'Their finest hour', Winston Churchill famously said of ... the RAF pilots who turned back the Luftwaffe again and again in the 'Battle of Britain' ...

Laboratory were conducting radio-wave experiments and found that a passing ship was interfering with their signals and bouncing them back, in a truly primitive form of radar.

All countries were aware of each other's research, and a veritable 'Battle of the Beams' went on throughout the 1930s. Britain, however, concerned by the threat from a resurgent Luftwaffe, gave this research a higher priority than other countries and stressed its defensive potential more. In contrast, Germany's research was divided among the three military services and private companies like radio manufacturer Telefunken, and it concentrated first on the need for warships to 'see' through clouds. It also focused on the use of shortwave transmissions, which generally yielded poorer-resolution images. And Hermann Göring, commander of the Luftwaffe, was less interested in the defensive uses of radar than offensive ones. The United States installed a primitive radar station at Pearl Harbor, but unfortunately it wasn't up and running at the time of the December 1941 attack.

RADAR WORKS!

In 1934, following Hitler's rise to power, Watson-Watt was asked by an alarmed British Air Ministry, represented by Harry E. Wimperis, head of the Committee for the Scientific Survey of Air Defence (CSSAD), to look into a rumour that the Germans had developed a death ray that used radio waves to destroy buildings. Was such a weapon possible? If so, could it be countered? Two weeks later, Watson-Watt handed in a multipage report reassuring Wimperis that the idea was impractical. A beam might be projected at a plane, but the plane would only pass through; it would not remain in 'the most intense beam we could project' long enough to weaken the airframe, jam the engine or, he wrote, 'make the pilot's blood boil'. Moreover, such an intense beam, even if one could be projected, would be more of a threat to

Robert Alexander Watson-Watt
with his 'radar'

the operators projecting it than to its eventual target. In closing, Watson-Watt reminded Wimperis of his own, more practical, research: 'Meanwhile attention is being turned to the still difficult, but less unpromising problem of radio detection and numerical considerations on the method of detection by reflected radio waves will be submitted when required'.

Wimperis immediately phoned and said the radio-detection method was required—'now'. On 12 February 1935, Watson-Watt sent Wimperis a memo entitled 'Detection and Location of Aircraft by Radio Methods'. Wimperis asked for a demonstration. On 26 February, a Heyford bomber flew back and forth between the BBC shortwave broadcast antenna at Daventry and two receiving antennas about 15 kilometres away. As the plane flew, Watson-

Watt, his associate Arnold Wilkins and Wimperis's representative, A.P. Rowe, watched a green line spike and retreat on the cathode-ray tube. The tracking was unmistakable and clear even when the plane was 13 kilometres away. Following Rowe's report, fifty thousand pounds were allocated for the development of radio detection and ranging—later shortened to 'radar' by the Americans. By December, Watson-Watt had extended the range of his radar system to 100 kilometres. Work began on five tracking stations on the coast and a network of stations, called the 'Chain Home' network, which by 1940 would stretch from Land's End in Cornwall to the Orkney Islands off the north coast of Scotland. With the onset of war, Britain's Aeronautical Research Committee, under Sir Henry Tizard, quickly saw the immense potential of radar for protecting the home islands and soon gave full support to its development.

While refining the use of radar to detect incoming planes, Watson-Watt recognised that it was also essential to get that information to pilots and ground defences quickly so that they could respond in time. He streamlined the reporting of radar signals so that trackers' reports went to a central map room instead of to their home base. Observers then guided the flyers by direct radio communication.

Watson-Watt then assigned another young associate, Edward Bowen, to design a radar system that could be carried inside a plane. By 1940, Bowen had produced a ninety-kilogram, five-hundred-watt radar that fitted into a Spitfire or Hurricane. (Later, in 1941, Bowen would also begin fitting British planes with transponders, which emitted radar signals that identified the aircraft as friendly to other British aircraft—the so-called 'Identification Friend or Foe' (IFF) signal.)

These brilliant innovations would soon prove critical in protecting Britain from the greatest threat it had ever faced.

As the plane flew, Watson-Watt ... watched a green line spike and retreat on the cathode-ray tube.

GÖRING'S EAGLE DAY

After the fall of France in the summer of 1940, Göring convinced Hitler that the Luftwaffe alone could bring Britain to its knees. His flyers would totally overwhelm the RAF, he said, saturation-bombing the airfields, catching many planes on the ground and knocking the rest out in aerial combat. The skies would belong to Germany, and the way would then be clear for Hitler's triumphant invasion of the British Isles. Subsequently, the Luftwaffe would launch attacks on London and other cities, creating such havoc that mass hysteria would result and Britain would sue for peace. The onslaught would begin on 10 July, and Göring designated 14 August as 'Eagle Day', the highlight of the campaign, in which massive bombardments would hit targets all over Britain.

... Britain would survive, and for that it owed a weighty debt to a young Scotsman's curiosity about thunderstorms.

As the air campaign progressed, however, the German flyers became increasingly frustrated with their lack of success. Each time they attacked, Spitfires and Hurricanes were up in the air almost immediately, attacking from altitude as soon as the bombers approached, as if they had already been waiting for them. Göring had boasted that the RAF had only fifty interceptors left, yet the British planes seemed to be everywhere. The German planes also suffered from a limited range. When Göring shifted the bombing targets from coastal airfields and radar stations to London, pilots complained that they arrived at their target with only ten minutes' fuel left. When German pilots ran out of fuel or were shot down by the ubiquitous British fighters, they faced a grim choice: parachute into hostile territory and become a prisoner or take a 'Channel bath'. British flyers, in contrast, bailed out into their homeland and many lived to fight another day—on both sides, planes were easily replaced, pilots more precious.

Eagle Day saw radar and the RAF triumphant. The Luftwaffe's eighteen hundred planes flew thirteen thousand sorties that day, with Heinkels and Dorniers dropping bombs from altitude and

Stuka dive-bombers machine-gunning airfields and city streets. They extended their range well into Scotland and northeast England. But the RAF anticipated their every move, that day and over the coming weeks. In three weeks in August alone, the RAF destroyed 602 German aircraft, losing only 259. By the time of the great aerial battle of 15–17 September, after which the Luftwaffe onslaught and the impending invasion were called off and never revived, Germany had lost 2,300 planes, the British 900.

Radar had given Britain a hot hand that it never relinquished. The German bombing continued for three more years, and the London 'Blitz' of 1941 was yet to come. But Britain would survive, and for that it owed a weighty debt to a young Scotsman's curiosity about thunderstorms. Watson-Watt himself, accompanied by Bowen, would move in 1941 to the Massachusetts Institute of Technology to establish the MIT Radiation Laboratory, beyond the reach of German bombs. More than half of all later radar developments emerged from the so-called 'Rad Lab'. While there, Watson-Watt would even find his own weapon being used against him: one day he was stopped for speeding—by a policeman using radar.

FIGHTERS FACE OFF

Throughout the war, British Spitfires and Hurricanes and German Messerschmitt 109s and 110s duelled with each other across the skies of Britain, continental Europe and North Africa. The planes were approximately equally matched. The first Spitfires were powered by a 1175-horsepower engine; the first ME-109 carried an 1100-horsepower powerplant. Both early models had a top speed of 583 kilometres per hour and a top ceiling of 11,000 metres. Both planes were subsequently upgraded and later ME-109s reached 727 kilometres per hour and 12,500 metres altitude. The Spitfire was armed with eight .303 Browning machine guns, the original ME-109 with one 20-millimetre cannon and two 7.92-millimetre machine guns. As time went on, the Spitfire became faster and the ME-109, as its armour increased, slower. The ME-109 was considered superior above 6000 metres and the Spitfire, especially the later models, better at lower altitude.

Trail of the Comet

Dédée de Jongh and the Belgian Resistance

The man in the black beret looked behind him with awe and admiration. Man and boy, Florentino Goicocechea had ranged the mountainous Basque territory dividing France and Spain, both as a hunting guide and as a sometime smuggler. Its brooding peaks and yawning chasms challenged even someone as experienced as he. Yet, here was this tiny wisp of a young urban woman— an artist, she said—matching him stride for stride, scrambling in the August twilight over monster boulders and fallen trees, and edging along narrow trails where a single misstep might pitch her two hundred metres to the valley below.

And showing indomitable courage and leadership, as well. She looked barely twenty, but she was emphatically hurrying along those following her: a woman and three men, including one tall man who carried himself like a soldier, all of them fleeing Belgium and France and hoping to rejoin the fight against Germany, somehow, somewhere else.

That August day in 1941 was Andrée 'Dédée' de Jongh's first crossing of the Pyrenees from occupied Europe to the haven of neutral Spain. Over the next year and a half, she was to traverse these heights thirty-five more times, personally shepherding 118 refugees, escapees, downed airmen, political prisoners and persecuted Jews out of the reaches of murderous Nazis. The escape network she set up was eventually credited with saving more than eight hundred people. It came to be known as the Comet, for the dazzling speed and regularity with which it operated.

BEATEN? NOT US

Brought up in the Brussels suburb of Schaerbeek, Dédée trained
as a nurse but loved to draw and was working as a commercial
artist for an advertising firm when German troops crossed the
Belgian frontier in May 1940. She was then twenty-four, too young
to recall World War I, but old enough to have been brought up
on stories of atrocities committed by the Germans. From 1914 to
1918, 'poor little Belgium' had fought valiantly under King Albert
until the Armistice. When Albert's son and successor, Leopold,
abruptly capitulated in less than three weeks after his country was
invaded in May 1940, many Belgians were outraged, and vilified
Leopold as a coward. One of them was a patriotic schoolmaster,
Frédéric de Jongh. Another was his daughter Dédée.

Former Comet Line operatives
at a 1946 reunion in Ciboure,
in the French Pyrenees

Leopold may have quit, but the de Jonghs were not beaten and neither, they believed, were the Belgian people. Surrender or no surrender, they began looking for ways to support the Allied cause. Some wounded British soldiers had been unhappily left behind as prisoners in Belgian hospitals when the British Expeditionary Force (BEF) evacuated. So Dédée gave up art and began to visit the wounded men, sitting at their bedsides, changing their bandages, bringing them food and talking to them about their experiences and the war. As the men's condition improved, she and they realised that they were destined to be moved to German prison camps. Dédée saw that the hospitals were not tightly guarded. Surreptitiously, she began to smuggle men out of the hospital, placing them in the homes of sympathetic friends, where she furnished them with clothing, food, false papers and money. By Christmas 1940, she had organised a network of 'safe houses' spread across Brussels.

The route through German-held territory that Dédée and other Comet Line couriers were to follow many times was a dangerous one.

Friends and former schoolmates signed on as helpers and couriers. Young girls bicycled from house to house, bringing messages and supplies to the men secreted in cellars and attics. These comings and goings could not help but attract the attention of the omnipresent Gestapo patrolling the Brussels streets. Couriers were stopped and arrested. Several men who had slipped out for a breath of air or to visit the local cafes were caught and jailed. Those who had sheltered them were jailed, too.

One of Dédée's most faithful couriers, Nadine Dumont, was hiding a Scottish Highlander, Jim Cromar, who had been left behind after Dunkirk and had fled into Belgium. 'He's afraid we'll all be shot if the Gestapo finds him', she told Dédée. 'He's going to leave and try to get to Gibraltar. He'll never get there. It's impossible. We've got to do something.' 'Give me a few days', Dédée said. By summer, she had hatched a plan to spirit the men to safety. The Comet Line was born.

When she returned for Nadine's Scottish soldier, she carried under her clothes forged papers and a falsified passport, and enough money for rail tickets and meals, contributed by the director of her former advertising agency. With the help of her dedicated couriers, she had set up an underground railroad of safe houses across occupied France and helpers who would carry her 'parcels'—the code word for escapees—and deliver them to Spain. She had also rounded up seven others eager to flee. They planned to cross the border in two groups, then meet at the small village of Corbie in Picardy, on the Somme River. But when Dédée and her party of four reached Corbie, in August 1941, the others, who were under the care of her colleague Arnold Deppe, were nowhere to be seen. Surmising—correctly—that Deppe's group had been arrested, Dédée bravely pushed south on her own.

UNDER GERMAN NOSES

The route through German-held territory that Dédée and other Comet Line couriers were to follow many times was a dangerous one. At Corbie, the little group entrained for Paris, changed trains under the noses of hawk-eyed German guards and travelled 650 kilometres overnight to Bayonne on the Bay of Biscay. Next day, they moved further south to the seaside resort of Biarritz, then on to a smaller beach town, Anglet. There they were welcomed by the Belgian de Greef family, ruled by the indomitable matriarch Elvire de Greef, known as 'Tante Go'. Tante Go had organised an underground force of resisters and set up safe houses throughout the western Pyrenees; she had also wangled jobs as translators for her husband and son with the occupying authorities, so she was kept well informed. At St-Jean-de-Luz, a few kilometres down the coast on the edge of the Basque country, the 'parcels' were turned over to Florentino Goicocechea for 'delivery'. As a Basque steeped in that fiercely independent race's tradition of what he called 'the import-export business', Florentino knew all the hidden trails that traversed the Pyrenees. He also had an abiding hatred of Fascism. Basques had fought on the losing Republican side in the Spanish Civil War, against Franco's Nationalists, who were backed by the Nazis. Rescuing other anti-Fascists and sticking a thumb in the eye of the German occupiers and their French collaborators Florentino regarded as his patriotic duty.

The true border between the two countries was the Bidassoa River, a rushing mountain stream that fed into the Bay of Biscay. Reached by an arduous uphill climb, it had to be forded at night because Franco's hated Guardia Civil patrolled the riverside road during the day. On this August night, however, the Bidassoa

Prisoners liberated from Mauthausen concentration camp cheer their U.S. liberators—Dédée was among the survivors

had been swollen by heavy thunderstorms and was a roaring torrent. Crossing in the dark would be far too risky. The group waited for four days, using their meagre supplies. With the river remaining unfordable, Florentino led them upstream to a small, secret wooden bridge and to the final safe house in France, in the hamlet of Urrugne. There, they were sheltered by a farmer's wife, Francia Usandizaga, who was to play a prominent role in the French Resistance, as the last stop before the difficult border crossing into Spain. Dédée left them and found her way alone to the British consulate at Bilbao. There she obtained travel papers allowing her Scottish soldier to travel on to the British garrison at Gibraltar and a British guarantee of funds for further escapees.

With her troupe safe in Spain, she retraced her steps to the Comet Line safe house in Paris. The arrest of Arnold Deppe had unmasked her, so she could not return to Brussels without risking arrest herself. She remained in Paris, organising the Comet Line from there and returning repeatedly to Spain. Her father and younger sister took over the task of tending the Brussels safe houses, assembling 'evaders' and sending them down the trail.

With her troupe safe in Spain, she retraced her steps to the Comet Line safe house in Paris.

A NEW CLIENTELE

Initially, the 'evaders' were mostly escaped prisoners or Belgians wanting to continue the fight, plus a handful of Belgian and Dutch Jews hoping to reach Lisbon for a flight to Canada or the United States. But by autumn 1941, the Comet Line was presented with a new load of 'parcels'. The RAF (later augmented by the U.S. Eighth Air Force) had begun daily bombing raids on the industrial cities of northwestern Germany, following a flight path that took them over Holland and Belgium. Greeted inevitably by heavy anti-aircraft fire and swarms of Luftwaffe fighters, the bombers often headed back so heavily damaged that crews were forced to bail out on the return trip. Most crewmen tried to stay with the shattered plane until safely over Belgian territory, where they could expect a friendly welcome.

Couriers and helpers now watched for parachutes and trained others to bring downed crewmen to safe houses in the Belgian countryside, where the Comet parcel service would pick them up. These new charges required new tactics. Young men of military age, especially if they did not speak French or Flemish, and had British or American mannerisms, were sure to be noticed. Dédée and her couriers taught them how to behave in public, especially in trains. When the compartment door was opened, by a ticket-taker or German guard, the courier would ask an innocuous question in French, and the young man would answer convincingly *Oui* or *Non*, with a nod or shake of the head.

> The Gestapo and its security forces were relentlessly closing in ... Dédée's father, Frédéric, was arrested in Paris in June 1943, jailed, then executed.

The Gestapo and its security forces were relentlessly closing in, however. Dédée's father, Frédéric, was arrested in Paris in June 1943, jailed, then executed. Her sister had been arrested in July 1942 and sent to a prison camp. Nadine, her early and trusted courier, was stopped on a train with ten 'evaders' that same summer. All were lined up before a firing squad and shot; Nadine's sixteen-year-old sister Micheline, known as 'Michou', replaced her. Another courier, Elvire Morrelle, fell in the Pyrenees and broke her leg. Carried to safety by Florentino, she returned to Paris on crutches and continued her work.

In November 1942, the Gestapo caught up with Florentino as he was returning from escorting a group to Spain. He was shot in the legs, captured and taken to hospital in Anglet. A few days later, a man in a German officer's uniform stormed in, shouting orders in German to two gun-brandishing troopers, and snatched Florentino from his bed. The 'officer' was the resourceful Ferdinand de Greef. He loaded Florentino onto a stretcher and carried him to a waiting ambulance driven by the concierge of the Anglet town hall. Florentino was soon back on the trails.

ALTERNATIVE ROUTES

Meanwhile, new escape lines were frustrating the German occupiers. The Patrick O'Leary Line, named for a British soldier who first charted it in the autumn of 1940 after the occupation of France, helped fliers who parachuted into Vichy France. The 'Pat Line' wound through central France and crossed the Pyrenees at their highest altitude in the 3,350-metre Ariège sector; it also took escapees out through a religious mission doubling as a safe house in Marseille. The line was credited with rescuing nearly one thousand airmen, many of them American.

The Marie-Claire Line was set up by an Englishwoman married to a French nobleman, Mary Lindell, the Comtesse de Moncy. She personally led flyers to the tiny (and neutral) principality of Andorra, another smugglers' haven high in the mid-Pyrenees. The Shelburn Line collected downed flyers from Holland, Belgium and northern France and took them by boat from Brittany to England. The 'Shetland Bus' was operated by Norwegian fishermen who had fled with their boats to the British Shetland Islands after the fall of Norway. Operating mainly in the winter darkness, the intrepid skippers made repeated trips to pluck evaders, refugees and downed pilots off the rugged Norwegian coast.

BALKAN RESCUE

While the Comet and other escape lines were snatching downed flyers out of Belgium, beginning in 1943 Yugoslav partisans were also rescuing airmen, while conducting one of the most successful guerilla operations of the war. Chetniks under Draza Mihailovic and partisans under the Communist Josip Broz Tito tied down thirteen German and six Italian divisions with their stubborn fighting. Among the flyers they would save were an estimated two thousand U.S. B-24 crews flying out of Italy to raid targets in eastern Germany and Eastern Europe; airmen who had bombed the oil fields in Ploiesti, Romania, which were vital to the German forces; and others who had raided the slave-labour factories at Auschwitz.

As with the Comet Line, young women made up the backbone of many of these escape lines. Some were as young as sixteen, like Michou Dumont, who fearlessly led a group of eight on the trek to Spain. Indeed, women assumed leadership roles throughout the Resistance. According to one estimate, half the fighters in the French Resistance were female. They specialised in gathering intelligence that could be radioed to Allied headquarters. From a casual conversation with a German soldier, they could learn about troop deployments, upcoming operations, reinforcements and weapons shipments and radio the information on to London.

THE COMET FADES

On 15 January 1943, Dédée's seventeen months of success caught up with her. She had brought a group to Francia's safe house, and was waiting for a break in the wintry conditions and for the fast-flowing river to subside. Tipped off by a French collaborator, the Gestapo swooped in and arrested all of them, including Francia. To take pressure off the others, Dédée insisted that she was the leader of the escape line, but the Gestapo refused to believe that such a young, slight-looking girl could have been responsible for leading such daring exploits. She was packed off to the Ravensbrück concentration camp along with Francia, then transferred to Mauthausen. Meanwhile, the Comet Line was reorganised by 'Tante Go' in the south and Jean-François Nothomb in Paris, and remained a vital lifeline for Allied flyers.

Though weakened by maltreatment in Mauthausen, Dédée survived the war. She was to display further heroism in later years, working as a nurse in a leper colony in the Belgian Congo and then heading a hospital in Addis Ababa, Ethiopia. When she eventually returned to Brussels, King Leopold's son and successor Baudouin made her a countess. At the time of writing, she was still living in Brussels, aged ninety.

A Long Walk To Hell

The Bataan Death March

Lieutenant Ed Dyess of the U.S. Army Air Force trudged along the dusty Philippine oxcart road that hot day of 11 April 1942, barely able to place one blistered foot in front of the other, and keeping his eyes downcast. His uniform was in tatters, he had not shaved in days and was hungry—very hungry—and desperately thirsty. He paused to take a breath and to watch the column of worn-out American and Filipino soldiers staggering forwards ahead of him. Instantly, a Japanese guard pounced, screaming an imprecation whose words Dyess did not understand, but whose message was clear, particularly when emphasised with a sharp jab from a bayonet: Keep moving!

Dyess shuffled his feet and kept moving. Further up the column he saw another bedraggled soldier stumble and fall to the ground. The guard pounced again. More shrill imprecations. More prods with the bayonet. The fallen man did not respond, simply lay crumpled by the roadside. The guard did not waste more breath. As Dyess watched, horrified, the guard raised his rifle and fired three shots into the man's back. He kicked the body into a ditch, then motioned to Dyess and the rest of the column to get moving.

Seventy-eight thousand sick, malnourished, feeble and bewildered American and Filipino prisoners were being forcibly marched out of the Bataan Peninsula on the island of Luzon by the Japanese invaders. They had held out for three months against the stronger and much better-equipped Japanese, but on 9 April, the American commander, General Edward King, had surrendered, recognising that his men were out of food and

> As Dyess watched, horrified, the guard raised his rifle and fired three shots into the man's back. He kicked the body into a ditch ...

ammunition and so ill that they could scarcely lift their rifles, let alone fire them. Obedient soldiers like Dyess had accordingly raised their hands in surrender. Now they would face nearly a year of unspeakable horror. And Dyess's role in the events of that year would have important implications, lasting well into the future.

HE WANTED WINGS

William Edwin Dyess, twenty-five in 1942, a boy from the barren open spaces of west Texas, had always been infatuated with flying. He had built model aeroplanes, taken his first flight with a barnstorming pilot at four and cycled out to landing strips to watch Taylor Cub monoplanes and Waco biplanes land and take off. He enlisted as soon as he was eligible and graduated from flight training in 1937 wearing pilot's wings. With his short stature—he fitted neatly into a cockpit—plus his air of daring combined with coolness, he was a natural choice for a pursuit pilot. By 1941, he was being trained in the U.S. Air Force's newest and hottest pursuit plane, the P-40 Curtiss Hawk, the first American military aircraft that could exceed 480 kilometres per hour.

Dyess also displayed strong leadership qualities. In November 1941, only married a few days, he was appointed commander of the Twenty-first Pursuit Squadron and assigned to Nichols Field in the Philippines. Eighteen days after his arrival, on Sunday 7 December, Japan bombed Pearl Harbor. Later that day, 8 December on the Philippine side of the International Date Line, planes from Japanese-held Formosa (now Taiwan) attacked the Philippines, including Nichols Field and Clark Field, both on Luzon.

The Japanese raid destroyed thirty-two P-40s and fourteen newly arrived B-17 Flying Fortress bombers. General Douglas MacArthur, commander of U.S. and Philippine forces, had been notified of the Pearl Harbor attack six hours earlier, but somehow his headquarters had not alerted the air force units and they were

Captured American and Filipino soldiers on the Bataan Peninsula of the Philippines in April 1942 sitting ducks. Dyess's pursuit squadron lost all but three of its treasured new P-40s on the ground along with nearly all the B-17s. The U.S. Air Force in the Philippines was almost wiped out.

With 450 planes compared to America's mere surviving handful, the Japanese quickly established air superiority, and Dyess's squadron lost more planes. On 22 December 1941, the Japanese, under strong air cover, landed a massive invasion force and began to drive across Luzon, the principal island of the Philippines. Dyess and the outnumbered remnants of the Twenty-first fought back, dogfight after dogfight.

But these meagre efforts were not enough. With heavy air support, the Japanese ground troops came in great waves, their tanks steadily forcing back the American and Filipino troops. MacArthur declared Manila, the capital, 'an open city', and began a measured, planned retreat, known as the Orange Plan, to bring all his forces together on the Bataan Peninsula, bordering Manila Bay, to await relief. Eighty per cent of the U.S. force consisted of teenaged Filipinos with little training, ragtag uniforms, outmoded equipment and sometimes no shoes. They fought valiantly but kept falling back to predesignated positions, using the mountainous terrain and the jungle for defence. Nichols Field was abandoned on 10 December as too exposed to be defended; Clark Field followed in early January. The Twenty-first Squadron's few planes now flew out of two makeshift landing strips hastily hacked out of the rice paddies near the tip of the peninsula.

As the retreat continued, more units poured into the peninsula. Food and other supplies ran short. Rations were cut in half and the men were forced to forage for food; 'I don't think there was a monkey left alive in the jungle', Dyess recalled later. By March, the 'Bataan Air Force' had been reduced to nine planes, only three of them P-40s, patched together by cannibalising damaged planes. The rest were outdated single-seater P-35s with little body armour and leaky fuel tanks, plus one antique biplane and two other aircraft. Dyess, by now a captain but with no plane to fly and few pilots to command, was pressed into service as an infantry officer. It was an assignment, he said, 'for which I had no skills whatsoever'. He found himself leading a handful of untrained men so ill and enfeebled that they could scarcely lift a weapon or maintain a formation. Nonetheless, he and a group of squadron mechanics and ground crews engaged in a week of stiff combat, clinging to ground around two field hospitals near the tip of the peninsula overlooking the American-held island fortress of Corregidor in Manila Bay. On 9 April, they were informed that General King had surrendered and they were all prisoners.

The dashing General

Douglas MacArthur

NOT PRISONERS BUT CRIMINALS

The flyers had heard lurid tales of Japanese abuse of captives and civilians during the war against China, but didn't fully accept them. They were soon disabused of their naivety. On the morning of 10 April, Dyess and other American and Filipino troops were assembled along the jungle road skirting the peninsula's eastern shore. There they were harangued for an hour by a fat officer who, jumping up and down and shouting, warned them in limited English that they were not prisoners but criminals and murderers, and would be treated accordingly. There would be absolutely no holds barred. Japan, it was pointed out, had never ratified the Third Geneva Convention dealing with the humane treatment of captured soldiers. There would be no ground rules for them.

The guards patrolling the column mimicked their leader, shouting and shrieking at the prisoners and prodding them with bayonets. As a first step, they demanded that all prisoners yield their personal possessions. One of Dyess's fellow officers resisted giving up his West Point class ring. The guard brandished a sword and pointed to the finger. 'Oh, give it to him, Sam', Dyess said. 'It's not worth it.' But the officer's finger had swollen due to beriberi and the ring would not slip off. The guard simply chopped off the officer's finger and snatched the ring.

The sun was baking hot and temperatures climbed into the thirties Celsius. No rest stops were allowed and water was neither offered nor permitted. Some men had brought full canteens, but Dyess watched angrily as one man raised his canteen to his lips, only to have it grabbed by a guard who mockingly emptied the contents on the ground and tossed the canteen into the jungle. As the line straggled forwards, some men crazed with thirst plunged into carabao (water buffalo) wallows and gulped the muddy, smelly liquid. Some guards, smirking and chuckling, would allow them to drink. But as one man dashed towards a wallow, a guard corralled him, threw him to the ground and stabbed him—once, twice, three times—with a bayonet through the chest. Then he turned to the others, pointed to the dying man, and nodded firmly and warningly before kicking the body into a ditch.

There was little provision for food. After the men had been struggling all day without rest, Dyess got his first 'meal'—half a handful of wet, sticky rice. As the men straggled through Filipino villages, locals silently and often tearfully proffered cups of water, bits of fruit or sugar cane, often at the risk of their own lives. Some were struck, shoved or even shot by guards. Prisoners who could endure the torture no longer sometimes broke for the jungle, the nearby rice paddies or cane fields. A few lucky ones escaped. Most were quickly cut down by guards' rifle fire, their bodies joining the corpses already scattered along the roads.

After the men had been struggling all day without rest, Dyess got his first 'meal'—half a handful of wet, sticky rice.

TAKEN BY SURPRISE

The Japanese, it was declared later, had been caught totally off guard by the surrender and at the numbers of men involved; the military leadership had drafted a plan for handling prisoners, expecting at most forty thousand—half the number that eventually surrendered. Nor were they apparently aware of the physical condition of the troops, it was said. Their plan called for stops, rest, water, sanitation, medical treatment and the construction of fenced enclosures as overnight 'camps'. The Japanese, though, had expected the defenders to hold out at least until 1 May. As of 10 April, none of the planned facilities were in place. Despite this, the Japanese forcefully rejected General King's offer to transport the weakened troops in American trucks instead of compelling them to march what turned out to be one hundred kilometres.

For the Americans, no supposedly humane plan excused the rampant sadism of the Japanese troops, which they were sure was either condoned or encouraged by the enemy leadership. There was, it was noted, a Japanese tradition that saw surrender as a form of weakness. According to this tradition, the proper and glorious course when defeat was imminent was suicide; anything less branded the perpetrator unworthy, subhuman and beneath contempt. Any treatment of such a person, however brutal, was morally justified.

As night fell on that awful first night, the stumbling prisoners were halted and herded into a fenced enclosure patrolled by guards. Set up as a waystop, as per the original 'plan', the camp was far too small for the numbers packed into it; there was no place to lie down or even sit, and little room to stand. Men stood shoulder to shoulder, propping each other up. Worse, there were no sanitation facilities; with perhaps half the men suffering from dysentery and diarrhoea, the stench and filth became overwhelming. There was still no food, and only a few spigots for water. Pleas for medicine went unanswered. Medicines confiscated from the military hospitals, it was later testified, had been taken by the Japanese for their own use. Men slept on their feet and at sunrise were prodded into motion again.

After four days—'It seemed like an eternity', Dyess said later—they reached the railhead at the village of Bogac. Here, they were shoved into old steel boxcars that had been baking in the sun all day. The doors were slammed behind them with only a small slit left open for ventilation. The men were crammed in so tightly that some swore their feet never reached the floor; instead, they were held aloft by others. The sick died, gasping for breath. Others took turns at the ventilating slit. After seven hours, the train halted at the town of San Fernando, and the prisoners were forced to walk another thirteen kilometres to Camp O'Donnell, a half-finished Philippine military camp that seemed almost worse than the march itself. In this hellhole, surrounded by barbed wire and watched by guards in towers manning machine guns, there were still no latrines, no medical service and only one water spigot for tens of thousands of men—they began to line up for water at dawn and often were still waiting at noon. The men were, however, fed regularly, if meagrely, but for many it was simply too late. Dyess called O'Donnell the 'Andersonville of the Pacific', after a notorious American Civil War prison camp where many died. Many died here, too: it was estimated that two thousand Americans succumbed in O'Donnell from wounds, malnutrition and untreated diseases, especially malaria. At one point, 50 Americans and 350 Filipinos were dying every day. Eventually, the total American death toll reached ten thousand.

FREE AT LAST

Dyess regained a somewhat shaky health over two months in O'Donnell and then, with other Americans, was moved by truck to an old Philippine army camp at Cabanatuan. In October 1942, he was loaded into a prison ship and packed off to Davao Prison Camp on the island of Mindanao. Davao was a penal colony for the Philippines' most dangerous criminals, many of them serving life terms—'They were the grandest bunch of murderers and cutthroats I have ever known', Dyess said later, only half jokingly. It was there that Dyess began fleshing out an idea that had never left his mind since the Bataan surrender: escape.

Carrying it out took him six months. As an old Texas boy familiar with cattle, he was assigned to drive a 'bull cart' used to transport implements, supplies and other inmates around the camp. He had access to all areas of the sprawling installation, including fields where the prisoners worked outside the gate. He could even exit the main gate; technically, he was required to stop for inspection but he became such a familiar figure that the guards simply waved him through.

Dyess lined up a handful of confederates and, with the aid of convicts, began to assemble a cache of food and even weapons such as the bolo knives that were used in the cane fields around

'I SHALL RETURN!'

With his designer uniforms, trademark corncob pipe and imperious manner, General Douglas MacArthur became a hero to Americans. His father, Arthur, had been high commissioner of the U.S.-held Philippines and Douglas had first gone there as a young junior officer in 1903. After decorated service in World War I and a term as U.S. chief of staff, he returned as the commonwealth's first commanding general. When the Japanese invaded, he insisted that he would stay put. But President Roosevelt felt he was important to home-front morale and decided to lure him away. He appealed to MacArthur's ego by insisting he was needed in Australia as commander of the entire southern Pacific. On 12 March 1942, MacArthur, his wife and son, the son's nanny and MacArthur's senior staff were plucked off the Manila Bay fortress of Corregidor, taken by boat to Mindanao, then flown to Darwin, Australia. Macarthur stepped off the plane and immediately pronounced a stirring message: 'To the people of the Philippines! I have come through and I shall return!' Some hooted at his vainglory (including his one-time aide, General Dwight D. Eisenhower), but it struck the right note with Filipinos and the American home front. 'I shall return!' became one of the most famous (and parodied) quotations in history.

the camp. These he smuggled out and stashed in rice paddies beyond the fence. Two deft convicts specialised in stealing chickens, which they could trade for hard rolls and dried fish that could be stored. Dyess signed on two young Filipinos with knowledge of the region and a naval officer who could help with navigation if they should reach the coast and commandeer a boat. On 4 April 1943, a Sunday when there were few guards on duty, Dyess and ten others slipped out the gate and were on their way, almost a year to the day after the surrender at Bataan.

The escapees were on the run for six weeks, wading through paddies, hacking their way through swordgrass, swimming rivers and streams, often with Japanese soldiers on their heels. At one point, they were on the point of being captured by Japanese troops when a group of Philippine guerillas arrived, drove off the Japanese and spirited the escapees into the hills. Afterwards, they took them to U.S. Colonel Wendell Fertig, an officer commanding a guerilla movement in the Mindanao hills, which gave the Japanese occupation force fits and regularly radioed the American South Pacific command in Australia with intelligence on troop movements. In mid-July 1943, through Fertig's efforts, a U.S. submarine arrived on the Mindanao shore and whisked Dyess, U.S. Navy Lieutenant Commander Melvyn McCoy, and U.S. Army Major Stephen Mellnik to Australia. They were the first Americans to escape Japanese captivity and safely reach Allied territory.

THE STORY GETS OUT

The fall of Bataan and the torture of so many prisoners was, of course, no secret, but the most horrendous details of the Death March were still unknown. In a recuperation ward in Australia, Dyess filed a full report on his imprisonment and told his story not only to General MacArthur personally, but also to a *New York Times* correspondent, Byron Darnton. Darnton wrote as much as he could get through censors but died in a plane crash in New Guinea a month later. President Franklin D. Roosevelt then clamped a lid on the story, fearing that disclosure might jeopardise the lives of other prisoners and undermine efforts to persuade the Japanese to accept relief shipments for the captives.

In August 1943, Dyess was flown home and sent to a military hospital to recover from his illnesses and injuries. There he spoke to military authorities and testified in closed session to Congress about the hideous treatment he had received and atrocities he had witnessed. By now an air force lieutenant colonel, he was transferred to the Fourth Air Force in California and received his second Distinguished Flying Cross—becoming one of fourteen U.S. airmen to obtain this double award during World War II.

It wasn't until January 1944 that the War and Navy Departments issued a press release containing full details based on Dyess's narrative. When the story surfaced in newspapers nationwide, the predictable result was worldwide outrage. There were demands for revenge and strident and harsh U.S. condemnation through the International Red Cross and neutral Switzerland.

Sadly, the man who had survived the Death March became a casualty himself. Test-piloting a Lockheed twin-engine fighter, the P-38, he developed engine trouble over Burbank, California, and was forced to crash-land. Rather than parachute and allow the plane to fall into a suburban area, he rode it down into a field and died on impact.

At war's end, a U.S. Army special court convicted General Masaharu Homma, commander of the Japanese Philippine campaign, for the atrocities, even though he protested that he knew nothing of the Death March and that, if he had, he would have stopped it. The court decided that even if the commanding general hadn't known, he should have. He was executed by a firing squad.

The Man
They Called 'Bomber'

The Allied Air Raids on Germany

The 700,000 residents of Cologne had heard it before, but never in such horrifying volume. The great cathedral city and industrial centre had been bombed ten times since the war began, but on the moonlit night of 30 May, 1942, the all-too-familiar roar and rumble of approaching aircraft seemed endless. Huddled in bomb shelters and in Cologne's deep cellars, the residents listened fearfully. For those few outside, the incoming planes seemed to blot out the moon. And then the bombs began to drop. Soon, explosions and fires were everywhere. 'It seemed like a thousand planes', one man said. He was right. With his 'Thousand-bomber Raid' on Cologne, Air Marshal Arthur Travers Harris, chief of Britain's Bomber Command, was making a statement—an emphatic statement that would resound through the war and beyond.

WEDDED TO A CONVICTION

Arthur Harris was widely known as 'Bomber' Harris, and not just because of his job title. He was firmly wedded to the belief that bombing held the key to all-out, decisive victory. Hit with enough bombs, the Germans would give up quickly. There would be no need for an invasion or drawn-out land campaign à la World War I. Bombing without mercy would save Allied lives. 'I do not personally regard the whole of the cities of Germany as worth the bones of one British grenadier', Harris declared, paraphrasing a comment by the German Otto von Bismarck.

Harris had another point to make. He fervently believed that wars were fought against people, not buildings or territory. His opponents in the British high command advocated precision bombing of the enemy's war machine—bombs should be dropped specifically on steel mills, munitions works and railways. If the war machine were destroyed, the enemy would be defeated for lack of supplies. Harris thought otherwise. Industrial output depended on workers. Bomb the cities and their working-class neighbourhoods, he said. Saturate them with bombs. Concentrate on the labour force, destroy their morale and industry would come to a standstill. He was like the legendary American boxer Tony Zale, who pulverised opponents by concentrating rains of blows to the midsection. When asked why he did not swing for the jaw, Zane replied logically, 'If you kill the body, the head will die'.

Harris was known as a workaholic, who kept his underlings at their desks until late at night. Staff members called him (behind his back) 'The Butcher', not because of his bombing policies but because of the way he carved up his subordinates with blasts of salty language, of which he had a seemingly bottomless supply. Associates found him arrogant and cool, but much of Bomber Command swore by him. 'He did not suffer fools gladly', one colleague said. 'Of course, he felt most people were fools.'

STRONG OPINIONS

Harris was also a man of opinions that he didn't mind sharing. He had enlisted during World War I as a sixteen-year-old bugler, and said he had been blowing his horn ever since. In 1927, as an up-and-coming RAF officer, he was assigned to the Army Staff College, where he

A British Avro Lancaster on a daylight bombing raid over the port of Bremen in Germany

found that the high command, still dominated by cavalry officers, stabled, maintained and fed horses so that officers could go fox-hunting. He snorted that the army's commanders would only accept the tank if it could be trained to eat hay and defecate like a horse—only he didn't say 'defecate'. He didn't think much of the Royal Navy either. 'Three things should never be allowed on a well-run yacht', he said, 'a wheelbarrow, an umbrella, and a naval officer.'

As he rose through the RAF ranks, Harris came under the influence of Giulio Douhet, an Italian air-power visionary who preached that only heavy aerial bombardment, especially of civilian targets, would win modern wars. The idea was taken up by Professor Ernest Lindemann (later Lord Cherwell), Churchill's wartime scientific adviser, who pressed it on the prime minister. In February 1942, Harris had just been named commander in chief of Bomber Command. Lindemann and Churchill, who was desperate to try anything, called him in and outlined the new strategy. Harris quickly made the idea his own. He was going to destroy Germany's cities, terrify the population and win the war.

Early air raids on German targets had not been very successful. The RAF's bomber fleet consisted largely of twin-engined craft with limited range and bomb-load capacity. It was in the process

THE EYE OF THE STORM

A firestorm is a phenomenon well known to forest-fire crews. During a firestorm, the fire burns so hot that it creates its own wind system. The rising air currents in turn draw in more and more surrounding air, causing tremendous turbulence that can even produce small tornadoes or whirlwinds. Temperatures may rise as high as 1,650 degrees Celsius; the heat is so intense that surrounding territory is often set afire not directly by the flames themselves but by heat radiation. A firestorm's demand for oxygen and fuel may be so rapacious that people are literally sucked in and incinerated, as happened in Dresden and Hamburg.

of being augmented by four-engined Lancasters and Stirlings, but planes and crews were still being lost to fighter attacks, anti-aircraft fire and midair collisions. Appalled at the losses for little apparent gain, critics at the Admiralty and in the War Cabinet argued that area bombing of strongly defended cities should be abandoned. The bombers should be diverted to something with greater payoff, like the U-boat war in the North Atlantic.

This only spurred Harris on. He resolved to send masses of planes, a thousand at a time, to overwhelm the German defences and obliterate everything below. German tracking systems could follow only six planes at a time; each anti-aircraft battery could contend with only four targets. To prevent midair collisions, which often occurred when planes flew in formation, the bombers would adopt a technique called streaming, whereby they flew in a steady stream at preassigned speed, altitude and separation, following radio beams from the new GEE radio-navigation system. Laden with incendiary bombs, the planes would ignite so many fires that firefighters could not keep up with them, and drop so many high-explosive bombs that the fire engines could not manoeuvre through the debris-blocked streets. The raid would concentrate on working-class residential neighborhoods.

A thousand-bomber raid would capture the world's attention and also silence Bomber Command's vehement critics at home. He went to Churchill with the idea and got the prime minister's hesitant approval. To re-emphasise the numbers involved, Harris decided to call the raid 'Operation Millennium'.

Early air raids on German targets had not been very successful. The RAF's bomber fleet consisted largely of twin-engined craft with limited range and bomb-load capacity.

SHAKING THE TREE

But where to find a thousand planes? The RAF had only 450 active, fully crewed bombers, even counting dive-bombers. Other planes and crews had been assigned to Training Command for the transition to four-engine aircraft. Harris cut the retraining short and added the trainees and planes to his armada. He also recalled 250 planes from Coastal Command antisubmarine patrols, but at the last minute Coastal Command reneged and withdrew the planes, annoyed at Harris's grandstanding and upstaging of his longtime rivals in the Admiralty. That didn't stop Harris. He called in every novice pilot, whether or not he had earned his wings, and put him in a cockpit. By shaking the trees, as he put it, he achieved a total of 1,043 planes of all configurations.

His first choice of a target for the Thousand-bomber Raid was Hamburg, Germany's second largest city and chief seaport. But after three consecutive nights of heavy weather and poor visibility, he went to his second choice. Cologne was Germany's third city, sited on a bend in the Rhine River and dominated by an easily spotted and magnificent medieval cathedral with twin spires more than 150 metres high. The city was part of the Rhine–Ruhr industrial complex, the site of iron and steel mills, heavy-machinery and armaments factories and chemical plants, as well as vast docks for industrial barges. The cathedral alone was so well known that the attack was bound to be widely reported.

> On the moonlit evening of 30 May 1942, the grand armada set off from airfields across southeast England to converge near Cologne at midnight.

On the moonlit evening of 30 May 1942, the grand armada set off from airfields across southeast England to converge near Cologne at midnight. The first bomb fell on the city at 12.47 am. The results were stunning. While the city's residents huddled in shelters and deep cellars, Harris's vast fleet flew over at the rate of one plane every six seconds, and dropped 1,400 tonnes of high-explosives and incendiaries—a bomb every other second. Two-thirds of the bombs were incendiaries, which started more than 2,500 fires, 1,700 of them classed as large, and beyond the resources of fire brigades to combat. More than 12,000 nonresidential buildings were damaged or destroyed. Half the University of Cologne was destroyed, along with schools, churches, hospitals and banks. More than 45,000 residents were bombed out of their homes;

411 civilians were killed and another 5,000 injured. Harris could not have been more pleased: the British had lost only forty-three of the thousand-plus planes that set out, and the streaming tactic had worked almost flawlessly.

THE CATHEDRAL STILL STANDS

When the residents emerged from the shelters the following morning, they saw a vast wasteland, with only their beloved cathedral looming intact above the smoking ruins. That gave Harris something else to crow about. He had ordered his crews to spare the architectural gem, and it was a tribute to their skill that it was virtually unscathed.

Two nights later, Harris launched another Thousand-bomber Raid on the industrial city of Essen and its famous Krupp armaments works, but it was less successful. A thick industrial smog hampered sighting of targets and the planes, at the limits of the GEE system, became scattered and missed targets. The third Thousand-bomber Raid was directed at the port city of Bremen, and caused heavy destruction to its facilities. The Focke-Wulf aircraft plant was heavily damaged, and eleven hectares of the densely populated inner city were destroyed. By autumn of 1942, the U.S. Eighth Air Force had arrived at British bases. American Flying Fortresses and Liberators now pounded targets in Germany during the day, while Bomber Command continued to strike at night.

The merciless bombing stirred an outcry on both sides. Lord Cherwell and Sir Henry Tizard, head of the Aeronautical Research Committee, engaged in a spirited debate about saturation bombing, Cherwell defending Harris's tactic and Tizard arguing it had not been effective, had caused heavy losses and was not only inhumane but would inspire Hitler to retaliate—which he did in raids called 'Baedeker' raids, named for the popular

travel guides because they targeted historic cities. A Cabinet-commissioned study concluded that the raids to date had been disappointing, but that effectiveness would improve with the new navigation systems and more trained pilots. Churchill responded by giving Harris a knighthood. German propaganda chief Josef Goebbels vilified Harris as an 'inhuman butcher', and Harris replaced Churchill as the No. 1 villain on the German hate list. Typically, Harris was unfazed. He pointed out that the Luftwaffe had bombed civilian targets in London and Coventry, famously gutting the Coventry cathedral with incendiary bombs. 'Did they expect they could bomb British cities freely and their own would be spared?' According to one account, he stood on the roof of the Air Ministry during a retaliatory Luftwaffe raid and shook his fist at the sky. 'They have sown the wind', he shouted, quoting the Biblical prophet Hosea. 'They shall reap the whirlwind!'

In August 1943, he turned the whirlwind loose on Hamburg in 'Operation Gomorrah', his most criticised onslaught, eight days and nights of bombing. Eight thousand tonnes of explosives were dropped, igniting a firestorm that totally ate out the heart of the old Hanseatic League city. More than a quarter of a million homes were destroyed and an estimated fifty thousand people died; many were simply swept off the streets by the powerful fire-generated winds and incinerated, their bodies never found. The consuming fire sucked oxygen out of the shelters and people died of carbon monoxide poisoning.

MAKING THE RUBBLE BOUNCE

After D-Day, Harris would became embroiled in another rancorous argument with the high command, who wanted him to bomb ahead of the advancing Allied troops instead of focusing on civilian targets. He protested that the high command's strategy was a 'panacea' and a distraction from the real task. He sought to

Two residents carry their bicycles through a devestated Cologne after a massive Allied air raid attack 'make the rubble bounce' in every German city, and insisted his policy would so shatter German morale that the war would end quickly. To prove his point, he launched a massive incendiary attack on the medieval city of Dresden, which had been largely untouched previously. The city was filling with refugees fleeing ahead of advancing Soviet troops. Feeding on the close-packed ancient buildings lined along narrow winding streets, the resulting firestorm gutted the historic centre, claiming lives variously estimated between twenty-five thousand and sixty thousand, including refugees and wounded soldiers who had been brought to the city for treatment.

Despite this, Harris continued to insist that saturation bombing was more humane than hand-to-hand infantry combat, but, as the war wound down, the British government no longer saw it that way. 'What is the value of conquering and occupying a country that has been more than half destroyed?' one cabinet member asked. The public, too, turned against Harris for bombing fiercely when the war was obviously coming to an end. He was denied a lifetime peerage, which other commanders received. Harris remained defiant. He launched one more 858-bomber raid on Cologne, on 2 March 1945, four days before the American forces took the city.

There are still those who maintain Harris should have been charged with war crimes. But Harris never apologised or expressed remorse for his merciless bombing strategy. There is a story about him, probably apocryphal, that may sum up his attitude best. One night during the bombing campaign, he was stopped for speeding by a policeman. 'Sir, you shouldn't have been driving so fast', the constable is reported to have said. 'Why, you might have killed some one.' 'Constable', Harris is alleged to have replied, 'I kill hundreds of people every night.'

The Reluctant Saboteurs

Hitler's Secret Plan To Destabilise America

On Saturday 13 June 1942, dense fog shrouded the tip of New York's Long Island when the dark shape of the German submarine *U-202* surfaced off Amagansett Beach, 160 kilometres east of the Empire State Building. The hatch opened, and four men piled into an inflatable rubber dinghy rowed by two sailors. After some nervous groping in the fog, the sailors managed to steer the dinghy onto the sand. The four men leaped out and unloaded four large bundles. The dinghy spun about and returned to the submarine.

The men were left onshore to put into action a bizarre plot that Hitler believed would strike terror into the hearts of Americans and cripple U.S. industry. It might even, Hitler thought, persuade the United States to sue for peace. The four men were trained saboteurs—on paper at least. English speakers who had lived in the United States, they had been given a three-week crash course in the tools of sabotage, and trained in cloak-and-dagger techniques. Their assignment was to destroy American war plants and vital infrastructure—railway bridges, dams, canal locks, highways, power plants. The bundles they brought ashore contained TNT, explosives disguised to resemble lumps of coal, detonator cords, timing devices and more than two hundred thousand U.S. dollars—the equivalent of two million U.S. dollars today.

As Hitler visualised it, theirs was a grand mission, with a grand plan. But it began to fall apart almost the minute the dinghy touched land.

The men were ... to put into action a bizarre plot that Hitler believed would strike terror into the hearts of Americans and cripple U.S. industry.

Coast Guard antisaboteur patrols assembling at a port on the East Coast of the United States

A MOTLEY CREW

The collapse of the plan had begun even before the men left Europe. Prior to crossing the Atlantic, the would-be saboteurs had been sent to German-occupied Paris. There they drank wine and visited brothels—where one of them, considered a leader and who in training had proved himself the most skilled and dedicated of the bunch, contracted gonorrhea and had to be left behind.

The four who reached Amagansett—George John Dasch, Ernst Peter Burger, Richard Quirin and Heinrich Heinck—had been handpicked, along with four other men scheduled to land by U-boat at Ponte Vedra Beach, near Jacksonville, Florida, five days later—Edward Kerling, Hermann Neubauer, Herbert Haupt and

Werner Thiel. All had spent long periods in the United States and belonged to the German-American Bund, a supposedly cultural organisation set up to promote friendship between the two countries, which in reality had strong Nazi links. The men had been chosen by Walter Kappe, a former Bund leader who had since risen to a top role in German intelligence. His plan, named 'Operation Pastorius'—for the leader of the party of immigrants that founded Germantown, near Philadelphia, in 1683—attracted the attention of the Führer himself. Determined to strike at America's industrial might before it could be fully mobilised against him—and thereby undercut U.S. public support for the war, perhaps forcing America to sue for peace—Hitler seized on the plan as his own. He overrode objections from Admiral Wilhelm Canaris, the head of the German intelligence service, who did not want to risk trained operatives in what he saw as a harebrained scheme, and from Admiral Karl Dönitz, commander of the submarine fleet, who was reluctant to divert any of his submarines from their mission to sink Allied shipping. In response, Canaris, who was later executed as an anti-Hitler plotter, said, 'We will lose a few good Nazis then'.

Kappe's choices were a motley crew. Dasch, a former New York waiter and the leader of the Long Island landing party, was a highly-strung voluble talker who seemed unable to keep secrets. He had been a poor student at the sabotage training school. Burger, like Kappe, had been an early Nazi, but had been thrown into a concentration camp in 1934 after the Night of the Long Knives split the party; he bitterly blamed the Nazis for his wife's miscarriage at the time of his imprisonment. Kerling, the leader of the group heading to Florida, had relationship problems, with both a wife and a mistress in New York. He signed on for the mission in the hope of seeing both and sorting out his entanglements. Neubauer, who had married an American and taken her back to

Germany, had been wounded on the eastern front in 1941 and was still limping. The youthful 'Herbie' Haupt had fled Chicago when his girlfriend became pregnant. He saw the mission as a free ticket back to that city.

UNLIKELY FISHERMEN

After ten days in a cramped submarine, the Long Island party was glad to breathe fresh air and stretch. They had scarcely gathered their possessions and their thoughts, however, when a tall, uniformed figure with a flashlight confronted them. John Cullen, twenty years old, was a fresh Coast Guard recruit assigned to routine patrol. Why were four oddly dressed men, talking in a different language, on the beach at midnight?

... Dasch 'explained' that they were fishermen, on their way home. Since they had neither fishing tackle nor fish, that seemed unlikely ...

When confronted by Cullen, Dasch 'explained' that they were fishermen, on their way home. Since they had neither fishing tackle nor fish, that seemed unlikely, as even Dasch recognised. Sensing Cullen's disbelief, he tried a different tack. He thrust a handful of bills at the young man, urging him not to tell anyone what he had seen. Prodded by Dasch to take the money and run, the puzzled young man pocketed the bills and headed directly back to his station. But by the time he returned at daylight with other Coast Guardsmen, the Germans were long gone. Scouting the area, the Coast Guardsmen easily found the Germans' bundles (minus the money), hastily half-buried in a clump of trees. These and other clues—a German infantryman's cap, a packet of German cigarettes and a jacket with telltale laundry marks—were quickly turned over to the FBI.

Meanwhile, the four Germans had split into two pairs to make themselves less conspicuous. Dasch and Burger went to the Long Island railway station, heading for Manhattan. They caught the first train, debarked at Jamaica Station, and went to a men's clothing store. There they purchased snappy new outfits, including straw hats and hound's-tooth jackets, which they donned on the spot. Arriving in Manhattan, they checked into an expensive hotel and ordered room service, including a whisky-and-soda for each of them. On Dasch's instructions, Quirin and Heinck travelled to the city separately and registered at a cheaper hotel. The two pairs were to meet up next day at a Midtown Swiss restaurant, or failing that, at dusk at Grant's Tomb by the Hudson River.

Now able to talk freely, Dasch and Burger quickly realised their common opposition to the project and to the Nazi regime. Burger was still seething about his treatment by the Gestapo. He confessed to Dasch that he had dropped the cigarettes and his jacket in the hope that they would be discovered and the plot thwarted. That would avenge his mistreatment and his wife's miscarriage. Dasch had worked in the propaganda ministry after his return to Germany, and had become angered by Nazi policies. He was a loyal German but no Nazi, he said, and had also decided to blow the whistle on Operation Pastorius.

THE JAPANESE TAKE A TURN

After the bumbling German saboteurs' effort on the U.S. Atlantic coast, Japan tried its own ploy on the Pacific coast. At dawn on 9 September 1942, a Japanese plane catapulted from long-range submarine I-25 overflew a forested area along the Oregon–California border. A forest ranger heard a pop like a car backfiring, spotted smoke, which he attributed to a lightning strike, and sounded an alarm. Instead of a blaze, the fire crews found a smouldering crater measuring more than fifteen metres across. When the site cooled, searchers found the nose cone of a Japanese incendiary bomb, the remains of a far-out attempt by the Japanese to ignite a dry-season forest fire that would sweep the West Coast, diverting resources and spreading panic. Two years later, the Japanese were to try again, this time sending 9000 hot-air balloons carrying incendiaries into the western United States. No fires were ignited, but a picnicking party found a balloon hanging from a tree and tried to pull it down. The attached bomb exploded, killing five of the party.

After further mutual encouragement and another couple of whiskies, the two went out to find a secure phone booth. Dasch dialled the FBI New York office and asked to speak directly to Director J. Edgar Hoover on a matter of 'military importance'. The agent assigned to what was called 'the nutters' desk' dutifully replied that Mr Hoover was in Washington but a local agent was qualified to talk to the caller if he would leave his name. Using the code name for the operation, Dasch dictated a message for Hoover: 'I, Franz Daniel Pastorius, will try to get in touch with him in Washington Thursday or Friday'. He and Burger then went shopping, spending freely on wristwatches, jewelled tiepins, cufflinks, bathrobes and slippers and cigars. The two were so busy shopping that they forgot the scheduled meeting with Quirin and Heinck.

The other two had been shopping, too, and patronising bars. Heinck was a heavy drinker and his German accent thickened with every beer. Alarmed, Quirin decided to move from the hotel to a modest rooming house where he felt they would be less conspicuous. After Dasch and Burger failed to appear for the lunch meeting, Quirin and Heinck went to Grant's Tomb at sunset and the four connected. Dasch gave new instructions for a Wednesday meeting at Macy's department store. But Dasch missed that meeting, too. All had been warned not to contact or try to look up old friends and acquaintances, but Dasch decided to visit a club frequented by his old waiter friends. He sat down to play pinochle, rationalising that playing cards would have a soothing effect on his growing jitters. The game lasted more than thirty-six hours, during which he flashed his thick bankroll and dropped hints about how he had left Germany in a submarine on 'an important mission'. He won several hundred dollars, which helped calm him. Then, on Thursday morning, he departed for Washington, leaving a note for Burger to 'take care of the boys'.

When Dasch phoned the FBI on the Friday morning and asked for Hoover, his call was put through to the director's office, then shunted through four levels of secretaries. He was about to hang up angrily when agent William Traynor picked up the phone. Hoover had kept the saboteurs' landing secret—he wanted to make sure that the FBI, not the Coast Guard, got full credit if there were any results—and Traynor was one of the few aware of it. Traynor listened to Dasch for a few minutes, concluded that he was genuine and agreed to send a car to bring him in. Over the next six days, under Traynor's gentle but persistent questioning, Dasch dictated a 254-page statement. Fortified by whisky and expensive dinners, he talked and talked, loving the spotlight. Until then, the FBI investigation had seemed at a dead end. And the FBI were still unaware of the existence of the second landing party in Florida.

Heinck was a heavy drinker and his German accent thickened with every beer.

BLOWING THE WHISTLE

The plan called for the New York and Florida groups to meet on 4 July in the bar of the Gibson Hotel, in Cincinnati. They would then scout one of their targets, the locks on the Ohio River, an important transportation route. Between their arrival in the United States and that rendezvous, the Florida party, like their compatriots in New York, split into two groups. Herbie Haupt and Hermann Neubauer travelled to Cincinnati via Chicago, at Haupt's insistence, even though he had been warned not to seek out family or old acquaintances there. Edward Kerling and Werner Thiel went to New York City.

By the time the two pairs reached New York and Chicago, Dasch was in the third day of his marathon questioning. He had even displayed a handkerchief where, inscribed in schoolboy invisible ink made legible by exposure to ammonia, were not only the names of the conspirators, but also their families and other

Haupt, left, and Dasch, right, on trial

contacts. By noon of Monday 22 June, all seven conspirators and their families were under FBI surveillance.

The roundup of the inept plotters was swift. Agents followed Burger from his hotel to a Fifth Avenue clothing store, where he picked up his new sharkskin suit and met Quirin and Heinck. After the others admired his choice of wardrobe, the three parted; agents immediately pounced on Quirin, shoved him into a car and whisked him off to the federal courthouse. Heinck was arrested a few minutes later as he purchased a ticket to a movie theatre. Burger walked back to his hotel and was just trying on his new suit when agents burst in the door.

Dasch's handkerchief also led the FBI to Kerling and Thiel in New York. Haupt was tracked down in Chicago, having resumed what his mother described as his usual routine: 'going to bars, playing cards, going to movies, looking for girls'. The FBI arrested him, laden with purchases including a diamond ring for his former girlfriend, as he rendezvoused at a movie theatre with the final member of the group, Neubauer. Thirteen days after the first group had stepped ashore at Amagansett, all of the would-be saboteurs were in custody.

GUILTY—OF WHAT?

'Nazi saboteurs arrested on Long Island'! headlines screamed after Director Hoover called a late-night press conference to announce the arrests. Hoover also notified President Franklin D. Roosevelt, being sure to take personal credit for thwarting the plot. Citing wartime security, Roosevelt ordered the saboteurs to be tried by a special military tribunal empowered to assess the death penalty, thus bypassing the constitutional niceties of the traditional civilian courts. All eight were swiftly found guilty of espionage and sabotage.

In vain, the appointed defence counsel, Colonel Kenneth Royall, pleaded that the group had not committed a single act of sabotage, had not even rehearsed one or scouted any of the potential targets. They had simply enjoyed a holiday visiting old friends and touring old haunts and had lived high, wide and handsomely on Germany's money. 'Because a man buys a gun and talks about killing does not make him guilty of murder', Royall protested. Despite this, all were sentenced to death, though the sentences of the two turncoats, Burger and Dasch, were commuted, Burger receiving a life term and Dasch thirty years. Friends and family of the saboteurs were also jailed.

The six were swiftly executed and interred in unmarked graves, in a field reserved for unknown and unclaimed bodies. When Admiral Canaris brought Hitler the news, the Führer flew into a rage. But he didn't learn a lesson. In 1944, at his direction, another submarine landed two would-be saboteurs carrying explosives, a wad of cash and some valuable diamonds on the coast of Maine. And guess what? No sooner had they arrived in America and bought a few drinks than one turned on the other and told the whole story to the FBI.

Fighting to the Last Breath

Jewish Armed Rebellion in the Warsaw Ghetto

He was barely past nineteen when the German panzers rolled into Poland on 1 September 1939, but thin-faced, wiry Mordecai Anielewicz knew even then what he had to do. Word had already spread through the Jewish community in Warsaw about the persecution of Jews in Germany: how they had been stripped of their rights and property, herded into camps, mocked on the streets, forced to wear a yellow Star of David that made them targets for further humiliation and persecution; how many had fled or were trying to flee for their lives; how others had docilely accepted, or acquiesced in, their torment. If such atrocities could occur in Germany, thought Anielewicz, Warsaw's Jews, who comprised thirty per cent of the city's population, could expect worse treatment. That, the young man decided, must not be allowed to happen. The Jews had to defend themselves. They must fight back. They must invoke the spirit of Masada, where the Jews had made a heroic last stand against the Roman army after the fall of Jerusalem in AD 70.

Three and a half years later, Anielewicz acted on those principles, leading one of the most courageous uprisings of the entire war.

A BORN LEADER

By 1939, Mordecai Anielewicz already had a reputation for organisational and leadership skills. A poor boy from a working-class family, he had attended a Zionist-Socialist high school, which stressed Jewish self-defence, and joined a Zionist youth movement, Hashomer Hatzair. He quickly became a leader and after completing high school, devoted himself to travelling around the country organising Zionist youth groups. He was in southwestern Poland near the German border when the war began. Hurrying back to Warsaw, on 7 September, almost a week after the invasion, Anielewicz led a group of young people into Eastern Poland, hoping to travel to Romania and open an escape route to Palestine (then still under British mandate). The group was stopped and imprisoned by the Red Army, then beginning to occupy Eastern Poland, and Anielewicz remained in jail several months before returning to Warsaw. He went from there to Vilnius, Lithuania, then under Russian control, where a number of fellow Zionist activists had taken refuge. He insisted to the others that they must return to Warsaw, resume their educational and political activities and set up an anti-Nazi underground. Anielewicz and his girlfriend, Mira Fukrer, were the first to go back, in January 1940.

The Germans quickly clamped an iron hand on Poland's Jewish community. In October 1940, Hans Frank, the Nazi administrator of German-occupied Poland (known as the General Government), established a ghetto in Warsaw, where none had existed before. The Germans subsequently set up similar ghettoes in almost all major Polish cities, including Cracow, Bialystok, Kielce, Lublin, Lodz and Lvov. Having been deprived of their property and rights, Jewish citizens were forced to move into these enclaves, to be joined there by Jews from surrounding cities and small towns, as well as others from Czechoslovakia and Austria.

In Warsaw, a high wall topped by barbed wire was constructed around the ghetto, which had only a single, guarded gate. A curfew was enforced from 7 pm to 7 am; later the ghetto was completely sealed and Jews forbidden to leave. A twenty-four-member council of former community leaders and elders, the Judenrat,

They must invoke the spirit of Masada, where the Jews had made a heroic last stand against the Roman army after the fall of Jerusalem in AD 70.

was organised to form a civilian administration, including its own police force. The Judenrat was also compelled to provide a list of all Jews in the ghetto and to supply Jews as labourers when ordered to do so by the Germans.

Anielewicz immediately set out to organise a resistance movement. He founded subversive cells, taught self-defence to the young, held meetings and educational seminars and published an underground newspaper, *Neged Hazerem* ('Against the Stream'). 'Jewish masses, the hour is drawing near!' he proclaimed in an early issue. 'You must be prepared to resist! Those who are not able to put up active resistance should resist passively, should go into hiding.' After the Gestapo asked for and received a listing of all 380,000 ghetto residents, he harangued the Judenrat for being too collaborative. He joined a semi-organised body known as the Antifascist Group; it finally broke apart amid friction between other Zionists, Communists and Anielewicz's activists, but that didn't stop Anielewicz. He reached out to Polish rebels in the 'Aryan sector' of the city in an effort to cement an alliance. His first attempt failed, but he kept trying.

Conditions in the ghetto, meanwhile, turned from bad to hideous. At a time when German soldiers were receiving 2,613 calories of food a day, the ghetto ration was only 253—by most standards, not enough for survival. The inhabitants became gaunt, emaciated skeletons. In the crowded, unsanitary conditions, disease was rampant, especially typhoid. There was a steady succession of deaths and burials.

IMPLEMENTING THE FINAL SOLUTION

In January 1942, senior officials of the Nazi regime met at Wannsee, near Berlin, where they decided on what became known as 'the final solution to the Jewish question'. Europe was

to be completely cleansed of its eleven million Jews. Anielewicz was not fully aware of the meeting, but the Nazis' intentions were already clear to him: the Jews were to be wiped out. In response, he had already begun to assemble a defensive force, known as the Jewish Fighting Organisation, or ZOB, from the initials of its Polish name, Zydowska Organizacja Bojowa. He was making day trips across Poland to set up additional ZOB units in the smaller Polish cities when the Germans put the 'final solution', known as Operation Reinhard, into action across the General Government in March 1942. On 22 July, the Judenrat was told it must supply six thousand Jews per day to be 'transported to the east' as labour. The decree applied to all ghetto inhabitants except factory workers, hospital staff, members of the Judenrat and their families, and the Jewish police. If the daily quota was not met, one hundred hostages would be shot every day. Between 22 July

Families who had participated in the 1943 Warsaw ghetto uprising being led away by Nazi troops and 3 October, a total of 310,322 Warsaw residents were crammed into antiquated boxcars and transported east. The Jewish police themselves shipped off 64,606 before the German army took over the awful job. While many accepted the official explanation for the deportations, others were less naïve. They recognised the train trip as a death sentence. And word gradually leaked back to the ghetto. The deportees were being taken to a newly completed camp at Treblinka. There they were being exterminated in gas chambers.

Anielewicz returned to Warsaw in September and was immediately galvanised into action. 'They let us live only to make use of our capacity to work to the last drop of blood and sweat', he fumed in the newspaper. 'You must be prepared to resist, not go like sheep to slaughter. Not a single Jew should go to the railroad cars.'

More than sixty thousand Jews still survived in the Warsaw ghetto, workers whose job skills made them too valuable to be eliminated.

'Mordecai threw himself into the defence activity with all his zeal', his colleague Emmanuel Ringelblum said. 'The Fighters' Organisation was created, at whose head the coordinating commission placed Comrade Mordecai. He was the soul of the organisation.' In the entire ghetto, there was only one pistol. Again, Anielewicz reached out to resistance groups on the other side of the ghetto fence and to the Polish government in exile in London, which was planning its own resistance effort and partisan warfare. By November 1942, a trickle of armaments, weapons and explosives was being smuggled into the ghetto. Along with the weapons, the ZOB received advice and training on guerilla tactics. The twenty-three-year-old Anielewicz was named the ZOB chief commander. 'Do not go willingly to your death', he exhorted his young followers. 'Fight for life to the last breath. Greet our murderers with teeth and claws, with axe and knife, hydrochloric acid and crowbars. Make the enemy pay for blood with blood.'

THE FÜHRER'S BIRTHDAY GIFT

Other insurgent groups were forming elsewhere in Poland. In Cracow, a wealthy German industrialist, Oskar Schindler, saved many Jews by classifying them as essential employees, and a ZOB group made up mainly of teenagers, organised by Anielewicz and led by Adolf Liebeskind, stormed a café patronised by the Gestapo and SS, killing several of their targets. 'We are embarking on a one-way journey with no return', Liebeskind had told his young followers the night before. 'We are fighting for three lines in a history book.'

The Germans, increasingly pressed by Soviet forces in the east, where they were also reeling from the onslaught of the Russian winter, could spare fewer troops for policing the occupied territories and turned even more responsibility over to the ruthless SS and Gestapo. More than sixty thousand Jews still survived in the Warsaw ghetto, workers whose job skills made them too valuable to be eliminated. But then SS chief Heinrich Himmler decreed that they must go, too. Warsaw must be 'Jew free' by 20 April 1943, as a birthday gift to the Führer.

On 18 January, the Germans came for the remaining Jews. To their astonishment, they were met by fierce and organised resistance. Anielewicz, wielding one of the ZOB's few pistols, led the battle on the ghetto's main street. Combined with another force rallying from a side street, the ZOB drove the surprised Germans backwards until they withdrew. They returned a second time and were repulsed again. After four unsuccessful days, the Nazis gave up and stopped the operation.

The respite gave Anielewicz breathing space to prepare for what he recognised would be the final struggle. The Warsaw ZOB now had 350 fighters, and they were supported by a second group, the ZZW (Zydowski Zwiazek Walki), the Jewish Fighting Union, which brought the total force to 750, all under Anielewicz's overall command. With the help of the Polish resistance and contacts in the government-in-exile in London, the ZOB obtained handguns, rifles, explosives, grenades, two machine guns, plus ammunition. They learned to fashion and stockpile Molotov cocktails. Anielewicz built and installed fighting posts through the streets, in windows and on rooftops. He fortified many of the air-raid shelters that the Germans had allowed residents to construct—after the city was struck by Allied and Soviet bombers. By the beginning of April 1943, fully aware that it might be a fight to the death, the ZOB was as prepared as it would ever be.

DEFIANT TO THE LAST

On the eve of Passover (2 April), the *Waffen* SS, the elite military arm of the Nazi party, smashed into the ghetto to clear it of all residents and resisters and force them onto the Treblinka trains. Anielewicz's men responded with gunfire and grenades from alleyways, sewers, house windows and even from burning buildings. The fighters were now equipped with two machine guns, fifteen rifles and fifty-nine pistols, plus grenades and explosives, and put them all to good use, the machine guns, for example, commanding the main thoroughfare. They fought the trained German troops street by street and block by block; German artillery shelled the buildings, set them afire one by one and sometimes shot those fleeing the fire. Even children fought. When the ghetto residents retreated into the air-raid shelters, bombs were thrown down the stairways, resulting in more casualties.

At first, the advantage lay with the inspired ghetto fighters, but during three more days of bitter street fighting, the ZOB was losing too many men and running out of ammunition. Despite heavy losses, the Germans came back with tanks and armoured cars and finally called in aircraft. Significant resistance ended. On 16 April, Anielewicz issued what amounted to his last proclamation:

What happened exceeded our boldest dreams … The dream of my life has risen to become fact. Self-defence in the ghetto will have been a reality. Jewish armed resistance and revenge are facts. I have been a witness to the magnificent heroic fighting of Jewish men in battle.

A week later, he wrote to a friend, 'Our end is imminent. But while we are in possession of arms, we shall continue to resist'. Sporadic fighting continued for another two weeks. Anielewicz still led it, from a bunker beneath the uprising's command post at Mila 18 Street. On 8 May, German troops stormed the building and set fire to it, killing Anielewicz, Mira Fukrer and other members of the ZOB. Some of the ZZW managed to flee and conduct partisan warfare outside the city. On 16 May, the uprising ended and the German commander, Brigadier General Jürgen Stroop, crowed to Hitler, 'There is no more Jewish suburb [sic] in Warsaw'. An estimated seven thousand ghetto inhabitants had been killed and another six thousand burned to death during the fighting. Fifty-six thousand survivors were rounded up and sent to Treblinka. Only one ghetto building was left standing.

By the beginning of April 1943, fully aware that it might be a fight to the death, the ZOB was as prepared as it would ever be.

Anielewicz's body was never found, but his 'dream' lived on. While many continued to go almost docilely to their deaths, the young man's example inspired others, notably in Lodz and Bialystok, to resist, as he had said, 'with teeth and claws'. A few members of his allied Jewish Fighting Union escaped the ghetto fighting, and conducted guerilla-like harassment in the countryside. And on 1 August 1944, a year after the ghetto uprising, Warsaw's 'Aryan' Poles rose up against their occupiers, held wide swathes of the city for five days—defiantly flying the Polish flag—and continued to struggle for two months before finally capitulating.

The Polish Students Who Broke the Nazis' Secret Code

The Discovery of Enigma

The convoy set out warily from Halifax, Nova Scotia, on 16 April 1943, setting a course through the perilous North Atlantic Ocean, then known as the graveyard of Allied ships, the German U-boats' happy hunting ground. Escorted by five Canadian and British warships, the forty-eight merchantmen carried weapons, raw materials including steel, lumber and phosphates, and foodstuffs, all destined for the hard-pressed and hungry British Isles. The sea route from North America to Europe was the Allies' lifeline: if ships didn't continue to get through, the Allied cause would be lost. Recently, the German subs had been sinking Allied vessels faster than shipyards could replace them: the previous month, U-boats had sent ninety-five cargoes to the bottom.

This time, however, the convoy's commanders were ready for the U-boat 'wolfpack'. Fed a steady stream of information gleaned from German communications intercepted by Allied intelligence officers working round the clock at a secret installation outside London, the naval commanders knew precisely where the wolfpack was lurking and how to elude it. As the subs positioned themselves for the attack, coded messages repeatedly directed the convoy out of reach of the U-boat fleet. Under this guiding hand, the merchantmen steamed from Newfoundland to Iceland and Greenland, where they came under the sheltering umbrella of patrol bombers. On 1 May, they reached their destinations and sent a terse message back to Halifax: 'All arrived'.

The voyage's successful conclusion sent another kind of message to Admiral Dönitz, commander of the U-boat fleet: Allied intelligence was now dealing a major setback to their campaign against merchant shipping. March 1943 had been the highpoint of German success. At the end of June, Dönitz would order the subs out of the Atlantic and send them to the Mediterranean.

It had taken more than fifteen years for the Allies to break the Germans' top-secret communications code and learn how to make effective use of the information they obtained. The task had involved the intelligence services of four nations and work carried out over the length and breadth of Europe. But ultimately its success depended on the brilliant efforts of three young students attending the University of Poznan in Poland in the 1930s.

... naval commanders knew precisely where the wolfpack was lurking and how to elude it.

TOP OF THE CLASS

Cloak-and-dagger work wasn't exactly what the three young men had in mind when they enrolled in the university in 1929. Marian Rejewski, twenty-three, planned to work as an actuary in a relative's insurance business; he was a mathematical 'genius', his father said. Jerzy Rozycki, not yet twenty, just liked to wrestle with mathematical problems. Henryk Zygalski, twenty-two, wasn't sure of his future, but maths was his strong suit. In 1929, however, Poznan was the focus of a desperate attempt by Polish authorities to break a new communications code being used by their powerful and increasingly bellicose neighbour, Germany.

For a decade, Poland had felt itself under threat from Germany and the Soviet Union, both of which were still smarting over the post-World War I creation of Poland from bits of Germany, Russia and Austria-Hungary. In response to an arms build-up the Polish government had established a skilled intelligence service that managed to monitor German and Soviet military messages. But then, in 1927, the messages abruptly changed and could no longer be deciphered. Polish intelligence recognised that the Germans had developed a new type of code, one that the experienced code-breakers could not figure out. Instead of a 'linguistic' code based on words and phrases, like those used by most countries, it seemed to be some type of numerical code, machine-generated and built on mathematical concepts.

For Poland to protect itself, the code had to be broken, and clearly mathematicians would be required to do this. So Colonel Guido Langer and Major Maksymilian Ciezki, heads of the cryptanalysis unit within the high command, went to Poznan University and sought the help of its mathematics department. Polish academia had a tradition of excellence in science and maths, and Poznan was then renowned as a centre of mathematical scholarship. It was also chosen because it lay in what had been German Poland, and many of its scholars were fluent in German.

Langer and Ciezki set up a course at Poznan in cryptanalysis, the science of deciphering and translating coded messages. One by one, students frustrated by the increasingly brain-twisting problems dropped out of class. Except for three, who relished the challenge and solved everything thrown at them. They were Marian Rejewski, Jerzy Rozycki and Henryk Zygalski. After they had completed their studies in 1931, Ciezki asked them to join the cryptanalysis unit, called the Biuro Szyfrow, or Cipher Bureau.

A MYSTERIOUS PARCEL

The three recruits could not have been more different. Rejewski was short, rumpled and unprepossessing; he had outstanding mathematical skills, but had shown little promise in his other

German soldiers hard at work
on an Enigma machine

classes. The youthful Rozycki was a bubbling extrovert; Ciezki had to remind him repeatedly of the need for secrecy and that he was to discuss the project with no one. Zygalski, a quiet, salt-of-the-earth type, had a practical rather than theoretical bent. Although classmates, the three were not close friends and spent little time together outside the classes.

Prior to the students' arrival, the Cipher Bureau had received a lucky break. A large, heavy package had arrived at Polish customs, sent from Germany to a German company in Warsaw. It seemed to contain some sort of machine. The agitated would-be recipients, and the German embassy, insisted that the package be returned, unopened, to the sender. But Polish customs, puzzled, notified Polish intelligence. Watched by Ciezki, customs officers carefully opened the package, revealing a machine with a keyboard, a plugboard and a set of rotors, and a complete set of instructions. Customs held the shipment for two days while the intelligence service made photographs and drawings of everything. The object appeared to be some sort of cryptographic machine, and bore the name Enigma, but no one could figure out how it worked.

The Enigma machine was carefully repackaged and returned. But the information was to prove highly valuable. Having adjudged Rejewski the most insightful of his trio of students, Ciezki installed him in a third-floor cubbyhole in the Cipher Bureau's headquarters and assigned him to breaking the Enigma code. Using intercepted test messages, Rejewski was soon able to decipher a coded message, but he could not work out how the machine scrambled the messages. He realised that the Germans used a different combination of keystrokes daily to create their messages. This meant that there would be so many variables that it would take a huge amount of time to break each day's code. By the time a day's code had been broken, the information might well be useless, and the work would have to start over next day.

In 1937, France and Poland had signed a secret mutual-assistance pact, promising each other aid in the event of attack by Germany.

A breakthrough came when a German cryptanalysis operative, Hans-Thilo Schmidt, offered to sell Enigma information to French intelligence. In December 1932, he delivered the sequence of keystrokes for September and October 1932. Using this and some shrewd guesses, Rejewski established how the machine worked. With this information and the drawings and photographs made in customs, Rejewski and Ciezki went to a small radio manufacturer outside Warsaw and had him build replicas of Enigma. Later, in 1938, Rejewski built a machine to assist with the time-consuming analysis of the vast number of potential keystroke combinations that could be used to code each day's messages. Known as a 'cryptographic bombe', it accomplished the work of about one hundred analysts and shortened the time required to break the daily code to two hours. As a result, Polish intelligence was able to decipher all German intercepts and gain constantly updated information on German military preparations.

A MOMENTOUS MEETING IN THE WOODS

The three young cryptanalysts were subsequently moved to their own headquarters in a woodland south of Warsaw, near a village called Pyry. On 25 July 1939, Pyry was the scene of one of the more momentous meetings of World War II. In 1937, France and Poland had signed a secret mutual-assistance pact, promising each other aid in the event of attack by Germany. Now that it was clear that a German invasion of Poland was imminent, Ciezki and Langer urged their French and allied British counterparts to come to Poland for an important meeting. Rejewski gave them a two-day tutorial on deciphering the Enigma codes. During one session, two large objects covered with cloth sat on a table and at one point Ciezki dramatically whipped the cover off one, revealing the Enigma machine, the heart of the code-cracking effort. 'Where did you get that?' asked the awestruck Major Gustave Bertrand, the French head of cryptanalysis security. 'We built it', Rejewski said, then presented one Enigma replica to each nation.

Four weeks later, German tanks rolled across the Polish border; three weeks after that they were outside Warsaw. By then, the Cipher Bureau had shipped documents and equipment to France. Rejewski, Rozycki and Zygalski fled with thousands of other Poles towards then-neutral Romania. At the French Embassy, they were given falsified papers identifying them as naturalised French citizens, and rail tickets for France. Technically listed as Polish Army officers, they set up shop in a château outside Paris, then, after France fell, moved south to a villa in Uzès, near Marseilles, in Unoccupied (Vichy) France, masquerading as French businessmen. They also established an underground operation in Oran, in French Algeria, to monitor naval messages and transmit them to the British and the Polish government-in-exile in London. As the Vichy government cooperated closely with the Germans, the Poles escaped from France over the Pyrenees into supposedly neutral but in reality Nazi-sympathising Spain. There they were imprisoned and tortured but finally with help from the British and the International Red Cross, reached Portugal, were taken

A CLEVER TRICK AT MIDWAY

Thanks to the code-breakers, the U.S. Navy knew before the battle of Midway that the Japanese were heading east across the Pacific in May 1942. But where were they going? Many thought the Aleutians, but Commander Joseph John Rochefort, head of cryptanalysis at fleet headquarters, thought Midway, and developed a trick to find out. He sent a secret message to the commander at Midway, asking him to respond, on an open circuit, that the island's freshwater distillation plant had broken. He suspected the code name for Midway was 'AF'. Next day, intercepts picked up a message from Tokyo to the Japanese commander that 'AF' was low on water. That confirmed the target. The code-breakers continued to intercept messages thereafter, giving the Navy an advantage in a battle that helped turn the war around.

to Gibraltar in a fishing boat and were airlifted from there to London. Sadly, Rozycki died in January 1942, when a ship he was travelling on sank during a storm, near the Balearic Islands.

FROM ENIGMA TO ULTRA

In September 1939, the British had established their own super-secret code-breaking headquarters at Bletchley Park, an estate eighty kilometres north of London. They had already incorporated the Poles' research into their own decoding efforts, but when Rejewski and Zygalski arrived they froze them out, possibly through arrogance or jealousy, or simply because of the language and cultural barrier. The two innovators were instead assigned to a signals company in the Polish government-in-exile and confined to decoding low-level ciphers. 'It was not one of Britain's finest hours', the historian David Kahn has written.

Bletchley Park, however, became a top-priority project and, despite its size and complexity, one of the best-kept and most closely guarded secrets of the war. Ten thousand cryptanalysts, mathematicians, physicists, chess wizards and puzzle mavens worked around the clock to decipher coded messages quickly, so that they would be useful to armies and fleets in minutes, not days. Code-named 'Ultra', because it was more than Top Secret, the project was soon decoding more than 2000 messages a day, including some from Hitler to his field commanders and diplomatic correspondence between Berlin and Tokyo. One of the Ultra team, Alan Turing, did vital work that not only greatly accelerated the decoding process (to the point that some commanders complained they were receiving too much information), but also led ultimately to the birth of the modern computer.

Ultra information proved critical in a variety of campaigns. In North Africa, for instance, after General Bernard Montgomery's victory at El Alamein, Rommel's *Afrika Korps* pulled back into

At the French Embassy, they were given falsified papers identifying them as naturalised French citizens, and rail tickets for France.

the French colony of Tunisia, where it badly bloodied the inexperienced American forces at Kasserine Pass on 14 February 1943. Rommel then retreated behind old French fortifications known as the Mareth Line. Decoded messages told Montgomery that Rommel was planning a counterattack at Medinine, twenty-five kilometres south of the Mareth Line. The messages disclosed the exact points of attack, the number of tanks deployed and the divisions that would be used. This gave Montgomery time to muster six hundred antitank guns, which were waiting for Rommel when he advanced. The massed guns blew away fifty tanks in short order, achieving a resounding victory. Rommel left Africa three days later.

Allied knowledge of Enigma also helped in the war in the Pacific. The Germans had furnished an Enigma machine to the Japanese, who had adapted it to create their own code, later known as 'Purple'. Using information from the British and Poles, U.S. intelligence services broke these codes before Pearl Harbor, though they were unable to decode messages fast enough to take action against that attack. However, as U.S. cryptanalysis methods improved, the acquired intelligence became more and more useful. Intercepted 'Purple' messages led to the ambush of Admiral Yamamoto's aircraft by a squadron of U.S. P-38 fighters and provided detailed information on Japanese fleet movements that gave the U.S. Navy the upper hand at the battles of Coral Sea and Midway.

The intelligence gained from the cracking of the Enigma code would also prove vital to the Allies in the build-up to D-Day. Commander Dwight D. Eisenhower later declared that the cryptanalysts' information had been 'a decisive factor' in the Allied victory in Europe. At the very least, it was said, the brilliant code-breaking that had begun with three university students in Poland had shortened the war by six months.

'Long Live Italy!' the Son-In-Law Cried

The Beginning of the End for Mussolini

On the overcast morning of 11 January 1944, in the Romeo-and-Juliet city of Verona in northern Italy, a youthful twenty-five-man firing squad nervously took aim. Seated before them, tied to schoolroom chairs and facing a wall, were their targets: five former members of the Italian government who had been convicted of treason. All had asked to be executed facing the firing squad, but that request had been refused; traitors, it was ruled, should be shot in the back. Just as the squad commander raised his arm to give the signal to fire, one of the condemned, a tall, handsome man with aristocratic bearing, wriggled free of his bonds and spun to face the firing squad. 'Long Live Italy!' he cried. 'Long Live Italy!' echoed two others. The squadron commander's arm came down: 'Fire!' But the tremulous young men botched the first attempt and only wounded their targets. 'Fire!' screamed the commander again, but still, after another barrage, the five did not die. Finally, the commander came over and dispatched each of the prisoners with a pistol shot to the head. 'Shoot', the man who had cried out said, and then he died. Count Gian Galeazzo Ciano, a high-ranking Fascist and son-in-law of Il Duce, Italy's supreme leader, was now officially a traitor.

At a lakeside villa outside the picturesque village of Salò on the shore of Lake Garda in northern Italy, which had recently been proclaimed the capital of a rump Italian state, Benito Mussolini

> Seated before them, tied to schoolroom chairs ... were their targets: five former members of the Italian government who had been convicted of treason.

received the news with no visible emotion. 'Justice has been done', he muttered. Although for more than twenty years he had been the not-to-be-questioned head of government, he had been powerless to intercede on behalf of his favourite daughter's husband, a ruthless but sophisticated man who had served as his foreign minister and had been at his right hand for more than a decade. Edda Mussolini Ciano had written imploringly to her father the day before, asking him to cancel the execution. She had even promised to yield Count Ciano's diaries, which both knew—and all Italy believed—contained explosive secrets. But Mussolini was by this time a shell of the jut-jawed man who had once transfixed much of the world. He could do nothing. His orders now came from his erstwhile ally, Adolf Hitler.

IL DUCE'S DAYS OF GLORY

It hadn't been like that in the early days. Through the 1920s and 1930s, after his notorious 'March on Rome' coup d'état had brought him to power, Mussolini had streamlined a previously backwards Italy, famously modernising the roads and making the trains run on time, and basked in the admiration of other nations and individuals, who saw his Fascism as an antidote to Soviet Communism. The American publisher Henry Luce devoted the entire July 1934 issue of *Fortune* to an adulatory profile of Fascist Italy. And at the first meeting between Mussolini and Hitler, at Brenner Pass in 1934, Hitler was deferential to the Italian leader (who scoffed at him privately as an uneducated upstart yokel), and the two nations became partners in the Rome–Berlin Axis.

Mussolini's invasion of Abyssinia (now Ethiopia) in 1935 brought condemnation from the League of Nations, but won further respect, along with material and moral support, from Hitler. When Mussolini repaid Hitler by, alone among European nations, backing the German annexation of Austria in 1938, Hitler

Hitler was profuse in his gratitude. 'Please tell Mussolini that I shall never forget him' ...

was profuse in his gratitude. 'Please tell Mussolini that I shall never forget him', he told the emissary who brought him the news. 'Never, never, never, whatever happens. If he should ever need any help or be in any danger, he must be assured that I will stick to him, even if the whole world were against him.'

But as Hitler grew increasingly powerful, Mussolini became more and more clearly the junior partner. Ultimately, he was to be subjected to a series of humiliations, and repeatedly forced by the

Fellow Fascists Benito Mussolini and Adolf Hitler at a meeting in Munich, Germany, in 1937

Führer to denounce many, like Ciano, who had stood staunchly by his side.

A PLAYBOY AND A BOUNDER

A tall, aristocratic, well-educated man, Gian Galeazzo Ciano was the son of a war hero and early Fascist, Count Costanzo Ciano. After law school, he briefly worked as a journalist then entered the diplomatic service, soon building a reputation as an international playboy in Peking (Beijing), Rio de Janeiro and Buenos Aires. 'He was a bounder', said Lord Vansittart, head of the British diplomatic service, regarding him as the classic Italian ladies' man. 'But bounding is no sin in the sun.'

In 1930, Ciano married Edda Mussolini, Il Duce's favourite daughter. After a lavish Rome wedding, the couple went off to Shanghai, where Ciano was consul-general and their son Fabrizio was born. Ciano came back to command a bomber squadron in the war against Abyssinia and was then named Minister of Press and Propaganda. In 1936, he became his father-in-law's foreign minister, at age thirty-three. His first mission was to visit Germany and pave the way for a visit from Mussolini that would formalise the relationship between the two nations. Ciano was warmly received by Hitler (although he and Hitler came to hate each other) and he and Joachim von Ribbentrop, Hitler's foreign minister (whom he also came to detest), worked out the details of the relationship. Il Duce's subsequent visit was a triumph—which left him completely under Hitler's sway. He came home and began remaking his armed forces in the German model, even cartoonishly practising the goosestep himself.

Count Gian Galeazzo Ciano

At the four-power Munich conference in 1938, which dismembered Czechoslovakia, Ciano was Mussolini's chief adviser and confidant. In 1939, Ciano and Ribbentrop negotiated the so-called Pact of Steel, a mutual-assistance treaty binding the two countries to come to each other's aid in the event of war. By now, however, Ciano had recognised that Germany was top dog and could ignore Italy at will. Despite the Italians' prominent role in Munich, they were given just one day's notice of the German invasion of Czechoslovakia; when it became clear that Hitler was about to attack Poland, Mussolini could obtain only vague information about when the blitzkrieg might start.

Consequently, when war came, Ciano persuaded Mussolini to remain on the sidelines. But when Germany overran France in 1940, Mussolini desperately wanted to be part of the winning side. He declared war on France and England a week before France fell. Then, despite opposition from Ciano and his generals, he decided to conduct his own war—'a parallel war', he told Ciano. This decision led to the disastrous Italian campaigns in late 1940 in North Africa, where the British captured 275,000 Italian troops, and Greece, where tenacious Greek mountain fighters drove the Italians back into Albania. In both cases, Mussolini had to appeal to Hitler for help.

... Ciano married Edda Mussolini, Il Duce's favourite daughter. After a lavish Rome wedding, the couple went off to Shanghai, where Ciano was consul-general ...

A FAMILY FEUD GOES NATIONAL

'There are traitors in your family', Hitler warned Mussolini in 1942. After the series of embarrassing debacles, Ciano had been whispering with other disaffected Fascists about suing for peace. As early as 1939, he had reached out to Britain, seeking to broker an agreement that would stymie Hitler and elevate Italian prestige. Now, in mid-1943, with the Allies attacking Sicily, he began to look for ways to take Italy out of the war. Mussolini, however, clung to his belief that the Axis would still triumph. By this time, father-in

-law and son-in-law were barely speaking. At the importuning of Hitler and Mussolini's wife, Rachele, who had come to hate her son-in-law, Il Duce reshuffled his cabinet, dropping Ciano and downgrading him to ambassador to the Vatican.

He did not, however, remove him from the Fascist Grand Council, the small group that dominated the party and was ostensibly the supreme power in the regime. Moreover, Ciano's transfer to the Vatican united him with Cardinal Montini, Vatican Secretary of State and an advocate for peace, who would later become Pope Paul VI. As the Allies advanced on Rome, various conspiracies, some with the cardinal's guidance, took shape within the Grand Council. The conspirators went to King Victor Emmanuel and received his tacit, unofficial support. One member of the council, Count Dino Grandi, circulated a draft resolution calling for Mussolini's resignation and for the king to replace him as head of state with Marshal Pietro Badoglio, commander-in -chief of the armed forces.

The rumours of Italy's imminent collapse reached Hitler's ears and, on Monday 19 July, he summoned Mussolini to one last meeting at the border. He bluntly told Mussolini that he must stay in power but turn over complete control of the military effort to the German high command and grant territory in northern Italy to Germany. A shaken Mussolini listened without comment, then the two men parted. When he returned to Rome, Mussolini was notified that there would be a meeting of the Grand Council to consider Grandi's resolution.

RESIGNATION, THEN RESCUE

The session began at 5 pm on Saturday 24 July. Mussolini spoke first, delivering, in his usual fashion, a long-winded, bombastic speech. He reviewed past triumphs, accused numerous others of being responsible for the nation's plight and at one point angrily accused the council members, including Ciano—'you, more than anyone', said Mussolini—of 'amassing fabulous riches'. Grandi next spoke in defence of his resolution, then Ciano, in a quiet voice, delineated his affection for Mussolini but made it clear he would vote in favour of his stepping down. Mussolini made another angry speech and, finally, at five o'clock in the morning, amid shouting and arguing, a vote was called for. Only one member abstained; eighteen others voted in favour. Mussolini was out. That afternoon he went to the royal palace and formally resigned. He expected that he would be called back to power, but instead the new government kidnapped him and whisked him off to a series of hideaways, while Badoglio took over as head of state and began negotiations for an armistice. On 8 September, Italy surrendered to the Allies.

But once more Hitler lived up to his promise of 1938. He ordered German forces into Italy, causing most of the Badoglio government to flee. Then he sent his favourite commando, Count Otto Skorzeny, to extract Mussolini from confinement atop Gran

JETTISONING HIS JEWISH PRINCESS

The Cianos weren't the only ones close to Mussolini who were let down by him. Margherita Sarfatti was Mussolini's mistress, biographer and house intellectual. The pretty, red-haired daughter of a wealthy Venetian Jewish family, she met Mussolini in 1911, when he was the editor of a Socialist journal. Thereafter, she shaped his career while sharing his bed. She composed his speeches and is credited with formulating many of the philosophical principles of the Fascist movement. There was no tradition of anti-Semitism in Italy and it was not an official Fascist policy. But as Mussolini came under the sway of Hitler, the Germans pushed Il Duce to rid the country of Jews, and many Italian Jews were subsequently deported to concentration camps. In 1938, Margherita saw the handwriting on the wall and fled. Her brother, however, was sent to a concentration camp and executed. After the war, Margherita returned to Italy and built a reputation as an art critic; she was even depicted by Susan Sarandon in the film 'The Cradle Will Rock'.

Sasso, a high peak in the Apennines. Skorzeny organised a daring rescue, using three gliders and taking a kidnapped Italian general with him to make it appear that Mussolini was being moved on the orders of the Italian government. All three gliders were damaged on landing and could not take off again. Nevertheless, Skorzeny bundled Mussolini into a tiny spotter plane the Germans had also landed and, despite the overloaded plane clipping a rock on takeoff and almost pitching into the valley, flew Il Duce to an Italian airfield and thence to Vienna.

Hitler then persuaded a reluctant Mussolini to return to Italy and set up a government to rival Badoglio's. Il Duce went through the motions of establishing a new Fascist state, the Italian Social Republic at Salò, which issued decrees socialising factories, ostensibly dethroning Victor Emmanuel and declaring war on the Allies. The new republic professed to speak for all of Italy, but its territory consisted only of those areas in northern Italy completely under the thumb of the Germans.

Ciano protested ... that it had already been shown to Mussolini. 'But why didn't you personally inform your father-in-law?' the prosecutor asked.

REVENGE OF THE REPUBLIC OF SALÒ

Hitler was adamant that Mussolini should have those who had voted against him arrested and shot. All but six had gone into hiding or fled the country. Ciano was still in Italy, but had applied for visas to Spain or South America. The German authorities offered to supply them on condition he went to Munich to collect them. There, the trusting Ciano was quickly arrested. His father-in-law's government imprisoned him in Verona and ordered that he and a group of other conspirators be tried in Verona on 20 November 1943. It was a drumhead trial with a foregone conclusion. The prosecution attempted to prove a 'premeditated plot' of treachery against the regime, but none of the defendants would admit to it—including Ciano, the final witness. When questioned by the prosecutor, he said, 'I never imagined that the resolution would cause the fall of the regime'—meaning the resignation of Mussolini. The prosecutor pressed him, asking why he hadn't warned Il Duce about the resolution. Ciano protested that he had been told that it had already been shown to Mussolini. 'But why didn't you personally inform your father-in-law?' the prosecutor asked. 'In view of your personal relationship with him, it would seem normal.' Ciano responded, 'Mussolini, even for me, was totally unapproachable. For months I had been unable to see him alone'.

The verdict was handed down next afternoon. One man, Tullio Cianetti, was given thirty years' imprisonment; the rest were to be shot. Edda Mussolini Ciano's pleas to her father to spare her husband's life had fallen on deaf ears. Il Duce was adamant. 'Here there is neither father nor grandfather. There is only Fascism's Duce', he declared. Edda departed for Switzerland, taking the telltale diaries with her.

At 8 am on 11 January 1944, a German officer came to the prison to announce that the executions would take place within an hour. The condemned men were bundled into a car to be taken to Fort Procolo, a few kilometres outside Verona. En route, Ciano suddenly lashed out at Mussolini, condemning him to Hell. But when they arrived, he was composed again and a final photograph showed his face almost serene. 'We were all swept away by the same storm', Ciano told the priest who had come to his cell to administer the last rites. 'Let my children know I died without bitterness to anyone.'

There was to be no last-minute reprieve from Mussolini. And so, as Ciano's son Fabrizio was later to put it in the title of his memoir, 'Grandpa had Daddy shot'.

How's the Weather Up There?

The Allied Meteorologists who Helped Ensure the Success of D-Day

Monday 5 June 1944 was the original D-Day, the day on which the Allies had planned to storm Hitler's Fortress Europe, and 4.15 am was H-Hour, the time General Dwight D. Eisenhower, commander of the Allied forces, had chosen for it to commence. A million-man army had been assembled, and the first invasion wave of 170,000 was ready to cross the English Channel. Planes lined the runways, awaiting the signal to take off, strike and bomb. Transport vessels and warships were poised in port. The only thing missing in the days leading up to the invasion was cooperative weather.

The fickle Channel weather had to be just right if the long-planned 'Operation Overlord' were to succeed. The invasion fleet would sail at night to conceal itself, and moonlight was essential for air cover and parachute drops. Winds had to be less than twenty kilometres per hour to make boat and parachute landings as smooth as possible. Tides had to be low at sunrise for men to storm ashore, and there had to be forty minutes of daylight beforehand to permit bombardment of enemy positions. Visibility had to be at least five kilometres, with no clouds below a hundred metres and no ground fog, so that targets would be clear and units able to see each other. If this combination did not click into place, the entire invasion might have to be postponed for a month, when the same tidal and moonlight preconditions would recur. That could prolong the conquest of Europe into the autumn, even the following year.

On Saturday 3 June, the outlook was grim. That evening, Eisenhower and his commanders met in Portsmouth, England, to hear an exceedingly gloomy weather report. A heavy storm had already hit the frequently choppy Channel. Skies looked ominous, winds were blustery, seas rolled and lashed. Thick, seemingly impenetrable cloud cover hung over the invasion beaches. Air supremacy, so vital to the operation, looked likely to be compromised. Armed with charts and barographs, the chief weatherman, RAF Group Captain James Martin Stagg, said sadly that the dire outlook might continue through Wednesday 7 June. A shaken Eisenhower delayed making a final no-go decision until 4.15 am on Sunday 4 June, twenty-four hours before the scheduled start. But when the commanders met again at that time, the report was no better. Reluctantly, Eisenhower postponed the invasion for another twenty-four hours.

RAF meteorologist Captain J.M. Stagg

On the Sunday evening, the despondent group gathered again for another meteorological update. It appeared—*appeared*, Stagg stressed cautiously—from the wind velocity and barometric pressures in the far reaches of the North Atlantic that the heavy weather might break briefly on Monday afternoon, providing a thirty-six-hour 'window' before the next storm hit on the Wednesday afternoon. Eisenhower brightened, but Stagg warned that more information was required. In particular, he was waiting anxiously for reports from a weather station 2,500 kilometres north of Normandy, on the remote island of Spitsbergen, 1,000 kilometres below the North Pole. That could decide the schedule of Operation Overlord.

AN ARCTIC WINDOW ON THE WEATHER

Predicting the weather had always been critical to shipping, and in the age of flight it had become more vital than ever. Military commanders recognised its central place in offensive strategy after World War I, when the key role of air cover became obvious. At that time meteorologists began to understand the global scale of some weather patterns: that Caribbean hurricanes were born at the equator and that Europe's warm summers and frigid winters were influenced by the weather in the Arctic.

It wasn't weather, however, that had first drawn oustiders to Spitsbergen, the largest of nine islands in the Svalbard archipelago. Fishermen and hunters arrived first, pursuing cod and seals and polar bears, and then whalers, who came for their quarry then went home. In the industrial age, coal deposits were found beneath the snow, and an American, John Monroe Longyear of Boston, set up the Arctic Coal Company in 1906 to mine the rich seams. He gave his name to the islands' first major settlement, Longyear City, or Longyearbyen in Norwegian. In 1920, an international treaty gave sovereignty of the archipelago to Norway—at eleven hundred kilometres distant, Svalbard's nearest neighbour—while allowing ten signatories to the treaty equal rights to operate commercial activities, mostly mining. Later, the Soviet Union and Germany signed the treaty, too, and a Soviet state coal company began operations on the islands in 1931. By 1941, Spitsbergen had a population of 2,800—mainly Soviet miners who returned home during the five-month Arctic night.

In the late 1920s, Spitsbergen also became the jumping-off place for Arctic explorations and polar overflights, which led to weather stations being built there and on another Norwegian-governed island, Jan Mayen, further south but still five hundred kilometres inside the Arctic Circle. It didn't take long for the observers to recognise that Spitsbergen, assaulted from one direction by fierce

... 'a spirited little war' broke out, with the weather stations and a first look at weather that might determine battlefield outcomes in Europe as the prize.

Arctic winds and from another by the warming influence of a branch of the Gulf Stream, lay at a critical point in the development of weather patterns affecting Europe.

When Germany overran Norway in May 1940, the victors claimed possession of Svalbard and Jan Mayen, since they were said to be part of the defeated country. The alarmed British concluded that could not be allowed to happen and what the historian John Keegan has called 'a spirited little war' broke out, with the weather stations and a first look at weather that might determine battlefield outcomes in Europe as the prize.

THE WARRING WEATHERMEN

The 'Weather War' began on Jan Mayen. An island fifty kilometres long but only three kilometres at its widest point, it is dominated by a 2,500-metre dormant volcano and devoid of vegetation. When World War II broke out, the entire population consisted of the four-man crew of the weather station. Hurricane-force winds blasted all summer long, so that meteorologists had to rig a lifeline between their buildings and cling to it to keep from being blown into the sea. After the fall of Norway, the brave Norwegian weather crew continued to collect weather data but defiantly sent it to London instead of German-occupied Oslo. Britain decided these patriots must be kept at their posts, and sent reinforcements and supplies on a ship. Landing at Jan Mayen's forbidding coast, however, the ship ran aground and sank. Another rescue ship came and ferried off the sixty-eight crewmen and four weathermen, then destroyed the weather station to keep it out of German hands.

The British came back the following spring and re-established the weather station. Coded weather reports, at three-hour intervals, were soon crackling over the airwaves to London. The Germans picked up the signals and dispatched planes to bomb and strafe the installation. But the crews' Husky dogs heard the approaching

British Royal Marine
Commandos landing in
Normandy on D-Day,
6 June 1944

planes before the humans, their howling and yelping working as an early-warning system, and the turbulent winds tossed the German planes about, destroyed their aim and caused numerous crashes. Frustrated, the Germans abandoned the aerial attack and began to use trawlers outfitted with sophisticated meteorological equipment to make their own observations. The Royal Navy made short work of them, however, and the Germans were forced to rely on aerial observations by seaplanes, which, however, were frequently grounded by the very weather they had come to observe.

... Allies brought in a sixty-man Norwegian force ... But their boat became trapped in the ice and was a sitting duck for German planes.

The attacks made the British resolve that Spitsbergen must not be allowed to fall into German hands, either. On 25 August 1941, the former luxury liner *Empress of Canada* arrived at Green Harbour on Spitsbergen, escorted by two cruisers and three destroyers, and carrying a raiding party of Canadian engineers and a platoon of Norwegian infantrymen. Their assignment was to destroy the weather station, blow up the mining operation and evacuate the Russian and Norwegian workers. Over the protests of the Soviet consul, who insisted he must have written orders from Moscow to allow the evacuation, which he claimed would take three days, the engineers set explosive charges in the mines, loaded the evacuees onto the ship and completed the job in six hours. They also set fire to coal stockpiles, which in turn ignited Longyear City and burned it to the ground. Then they packed the Russians off to the Arctic port of Archangel, returned for the demolition crew and went home with plans to come back, like robins, in the spring.

THE GERMANS COME AND GO

But the Germans crept in behind them, with their own weathermen. They came to stay, bringing equipment to build a landing strip and weather station as well as erect machine-gun emplacements.

Another German expedition established a second observation station on the most remote northern part of the island. Both were immediately transmitting weather reports, using various frequencies to evade detection.

So, in May 1943, the Allies brought in a sixty-man Norwegian force, supplied by the Norwegian government-in-exile in London. But their boat became trapped in the ice and was a sitting duck for German planes. Fourteen Norwegians were killed and the rest left stranded on the ice. After two weeks, a flying boat arrived from the Shetland Islands, 2,500 kilometres away, and dropped food, medical supplies and weapons. A week later, as the ice began to break up, the flying boat returned with reinforcements.

PHANTOM ARMIES

At the same time as they were amassing their enormous Normandy invasion force, the Allies managed to convince the Germans that the offensive would occur in another place—or places—entirely. Their campaign of deception, known as Operation Fortitude, involved creating a fictitious American force, the First U.S. Army Group ('FUSAG'), which was supposedly commanded by (the very real) General George Patton and preparing to strike precisely where Germans would most expect it—directly across the English Channel from Dover in the Pas de Calais region. To make this convincing, fake landing craft were anchored in the Thames, inflated rubber tanks were placed in fields, dummy airstrips were marked off and lined with fake planes, and fake barracks, field kitchens and hospitals were constructed near Dover. Patton even visited the 'camps' a few times. Meanwhile, the intelligence services filled the airwaves with false radio messages to FUSAG 'headquarters' from imaginary corps and phantom spies. Other agents went around neutral capitals buying up stocks of Michelin maps of the Pas de Calais. Another imaginary army, the British Fourth Army, was conjured up in Scotland to give the impression that the Allies were also preparing to mount a diversionary attack in Norway.

The Germans fell for the ruse, becoming so convinced that an attack on the Pas de Calais was imminent that they posted the entire Fifteenth Army there, a force of more than 100,000. Two weeks after D-Day, it was still waiting there, its generals convinced that the Normandy attack was a mere feint.

They advanced on the camp only to find that the Germans, having learned of the Allied build-up through aerial reconnaissance, had left. The Allies had Spitsbergen to themselves. New weather stations staffed by Norwegians were built at Longyear City and Barentsburg, and were soon sending weather reports to Britain.

To Adolf Hitler, the withdrawal was an indignity. Apart from the lost weather data, he feared the Allies were constructing an air-and-sea base from which to harass German installations in Norway and thwart submarine warfare along the Murmansk supply route to the Soviet Union. So he sent two battleships, the *Tirpitz* and the *Scharnhorst* ('Men to do a boy's job', one British admiral commented afterwards) to the far-off Arctic to level the weather installations and teach the Allies a lesson.

On 7 September 1943, three German destroyers reached Green Harbour and unloaded a landing party, while the *Tirpitz* opened up with its fifteen-inch (thirty-eight centimetre) guns. The Norwegians, with only light anti-aircraft guns, fired a few shots and then withdrew. However, the *Tirpitz* bombardment harmed the attackers more than the defenders, the shells landing among the German troops and scattering them, allowing the Norwegians to escape. The *Tirpitz* then turned its guns on Barentsburg, but most of its shells landed in the huge ash deposits behind the mining installation and caused no damage. The *Scharnhorst*, meanwhile, attacked Longyear City. Its raiding party stormed a Norwegian battery, killing six and taking five captive, and the ship's guns then levelled the settlement. But at 11 am, as set out in the plan of attack, the raiding party returned to the ship. The flotilla steamed away and the Weather War ended.

Within weeks, the Allied weather stations were once again sending detailed observations to Britain, where they provided valuable guidance to the RAF and proved critical in the preparations for D-Day.

THROUGH A WINDOW IN THE WEATHER

At 4.15 am on 5 June 1944, the Supreme Command met again.

A stiff wind was shaking the little camp as they gathered, and the rain, Eisenhower was to write later, 'seemed to be travelling in horizontal streaks'. Just looking out the window, he said, 'it seemed impossible in such conditions that there was any reason for even discussing the situation'. Then Stagg arrived with his armload of information. Observations of wind, temperature and barometric pressure all the way up to the Arctic, he said, indicated that the storm would abate before the morning of 6 June and a calm interlude would follow. In particular, the weather report from Spitsbergen had reinforced his optimistic outlook. Stagg looked at the others, who had been sitting tensely while he spoke. Then Eisenhower relaxed and beamed his famous grin. He turned to the Allied deputy commander, British General Bernard Law Montgomery. 'Okay', he said. 'We'll go.'

At dawn on 6 June 1944, the first Allied troops sailed over a relatively calm English Channel and tromped ashore on the Normandy beaches under cloudy but rainless skies, in moderate winds—just as the forecasters had predicted. By nightfall, well over one hundred thousand men had established a foothold on the Normandy beaches, opening the way for a difficult but successful ten-month drive towards Berlin. The Germans, in contrast, had relaxed their guard, concluding, after peering at the brooding skies and studying their own faulty and fragmented forecasts, that no invasion was likely in such forbidding conditions. Field Marshal Rommel had even gone on a few days' leave.

Eisenhower had made the right decision, and for that he and the Allies could thank a handful of intrepid men who had fought a tenacious battle, in extreme weather conditions, on some of the most inhospitable territory on Earth, to preserve a distant and tiny, but vital, outpost.

... Allied weather stations were ... sending detailed observations to Britain, where they provided valuable guidance to the RAF and proved critical in the preparations for D-Day.

'Go For Broke'

The Allies' Japanese-American Heroes

Twenty-two-year-old Private Joe Sakato fired burst after burst from his Thompson submachine gun, trying to quell his anger. His best friend had just died in his arms from a German bullet. Sakato beckoned to his platoon: 'Come on!' He dashed towards the Germans, blazing away with his 'Tommy gun' until he had expended both clips of cartridges, snatched up a wounded soldier's rifle and emptied that, then fired a P-38 pistol he had taken in a foxhole. Inspired by his example, his platoon mates charged. A handful of unwounded Germans turned and fled in bewilderment. They had just been routed by a banzai charge—'one of the first in American military history', as Sakato was to say later. For Sakato and the other men of the 442nd Regimental Combat Team were all Japanese-Americans, many of whose families were confined in 'relocation camps' in desolate parts of America as potential enemies.

The 'Four-four-two', with its slogan 'Go for Broke', had been tapped to lead a last-ditch effort, in October 1944, to save a 'Lost Battalion' trapped behind enemy lines in the Vosges region of France. After a heroic record during the invasion of Sicily, the siege of Monte Cassino and the Anzio beachhead in Italy, it had seemed a logical choice. It was a mission that would cement the 442nd's reputation as the most decorated outfit in the U.S. Army.

ENEMIES EVERYWHERE

After Pearl Harbor, something akin to panic had swept parts of the United States. Anyone with Asian features was branded an enemy and a possible spy or saboteur. No matter that many of these 'enemies' had lived in the United States for decades and some were American citizens. Just the colour of their skin made them a threat, the scare story went.

Japanese and those of Japanese descent, 150,000 strong, comprised almost half the population of Hawaii; there were 110,000 in California and another cluster in the state of Washington. Many were first-generation immigrants, known as 'Issei', but others, including many young men of draft age, were American-born 'Nisei', and citizens by birth. Nevertheless, on orders of President Roosevelt and with the tacit approval of Secretary of War Henry Stimson, Lieutenant General John L. DeWitt, the military commander of the Western Defence Command and Fourth Army, decreed that all Japanese and 'American citizens of Japanese lineage' must be promptly 'excluded' from what were termed 'war zones' around major cities and along the coast. They might, after all, collaborate with invaders or commit acts of terror. 'A Jap is a Jap', DeWitt said, when told that many were citizens and the decree might violate their constitutional rights. 'It is impossible to estimate who is loyal or disloyal with any degree of safety.' Chinese, Koreans and Filipinos were caught up in the panic, too.

In February 1942, two months after Pearl Harbor, Roosevelt signed the 'exclusion order', and a huge exodus began. Whole families were uprooted, forced to sell or simply give up their homes, quit jobs, sacrifice businesses they had built up over years, pack one suitcase per person and head for parts of the country they had never seen or even heard of—places as remote as the Ozark Mountains of Arkansas, the northeastern California high desert and the Rockies of Idaho. There they were housed in makeshift camps with common latrines, hastily thrown up or converted from old Civilian Conservation Corps installations. As unforgettably described by Jeanne Wakatsuki Houston, a child of the camps, in *Farewell to Manzanar*, they were expected to conduct normal

He dashed towards the Germans, blazing away with his 'Tommy gun' until he had expended both clips of cartridges, snatched up a wounded soldier's rifle and emptied that, then fired a P-38 pistol he had taken in a foxhole.

lives and raise children, to 'organise self-supporting and self-administered communities'. And, of course, support the war.

Among those 'relocated' was the family of Joe Sakato. The Sakatos had for years operated a small butcher shop and fruit stand in Colton, in San Bernardino County, California, east of Los Angeles. They had just purchased a new state-of-the-art refrigerator for eight hundred dollars, a huge sum in 1941. They were forced to sell it for five hundred—and 'throw in the rest of the store with it', Sakato said. As part of the initial 'voluntary relocation' policy, they packed what they could into a borrowed truck and migrated to Glendale, Arizona, where a relative lived. The next stop was to be the Poston Relocation Centre, 250 kilometres away, in Arizona's western desert, near the California border.

ROUNDING UP THE NO-NOS

Authorities in Hawaii, despite being closer to Japan, were more lenient. Even though the islands were still under martial law, officials could see no military necessity for the evacuation of Japanese-Americans. Besides, housing and guarding them would be a huge expense, and a loss to the community; the Japanese were vital to the economy, including the military bases, where many worked.

The young Japanese-American men of Hawaii were baffled by the new restrictions. They felt no kinship with the Asian Japanese; they were Americans, after all, and wanted to enlist and fight like other Americans. Some, indeed, already had military experience and had served in the Hawaii National Guard, even the college Reserve Officers Training Corps, where they won commissions. Yet they were prohibited from serving and were classified as 'IV-C'—undraftable. In 1943, however, the rules changed and Japanese-Americans born under the U.S. flag were encouraged to volunteer. A quota of fifteen hundred was set for Hawaii; an astonishing ten thousand stepped forward eagerly, proving that to them America came first. They were quickly mobilised into the all-Nisei (except for white officers) 100th Infantry Battalion (Separate), the 'separate' indicating that they were not part of a division or regiment—a new category for the army.

Things were different among the mainland Nisei, however. They were assigned a quota of 3000, but only 1208 volunteered. There, General DeWitt had decreed that the volunteers must complete a 'loyalty questionnaire', asking if they would serve willingly in the armed forces, swear unqualified allegiance to the U.S. and forswear allegiance and obedience to the Japanese emperor. Many Japanese-Americans were outraged by the clumsily written questionnaire: they were being asked if they would serve a country that, in their view, had just deprived them and their families of their constitutional rights and freedoms and their property, and made them second-class citizens, and to renounce allegiance to an emperor to whom they had never sworn allegiance in the first place. Consequently, many volunteers refused to sign the questionnaire. Dubbed 'No-nos', or 'segregees', they were rounded up, loaded onto trains, and taken to the most remote and dismal relocation centre of all, Tule Lake, in the isolated lava-bed country on the California–Oregon boundary. Those who had signed were formed into a basic-training unit.

THE NISEI IN ACTION

At first, to the anger of many in Hawaii's 100th Battalion, they were restricted to guard duty. Then, under pressure from General Mark Clark, who would later command them in Italy, the Hawaiian and mainland groups were merged into an unprecedented organisation, designated the 442nd Regimental Combat Team. The 442nd consisted of three infantry battalions, including Hawaii's 100th Battalion, which was permitted to keep its identity (members nicknamed it the 'One Puka-Puka', *puka* being a Hawaiian-Japanese slang term for 'zero'); an artillery battalion; and an antitank unit. Green though it was, the 442nd went ashore in Sicily in July 1943, and built a reputation as an elite unit, fighting up the Italian boot, most notably at Monte Cassino and Anzio, and finally marching into Rome.

Joe Sakato didn't go into action until 15 October 1944. He had tried for the Army Air Corps and been rejected, and had then been drafted and assigned with his friend Saburo Tanamachi to the 442nd as an infantry replacement. 'After Italy, [the 442nd] needed replacements [for the casualties] so they scrounged the whole army and anyone with a Japanese name went into combat training', said another replacement, Shig Doi, who had been a technician in a military dental clinic before suddenly finding himself in the infantry.

In the summer of 1944, about a hundred young Nisei were shipped across the ocean to Italy as 442 replacements, just as the U.S. Seventh Army invaded southern France. In what was called Operation Anvil and then Operation Dragoon, the Seventh was to drive north up the Rhône River valley and unite with the D-Day armies sweeping east from Normandy. The operation was to be spearheaded by some of the army's most seasoned troops, including the 442nd, and the Thirty-sixth and Forty-fifth Divisions, veterans of the North African and Italian campaigns. By October, this army had punched 560 kilometres into France. The 442nd fought a savage battle at a small town, Bruyères, where Sakato, tasting battle for the first time, earned the name 'Machine-gun Joe' for his relentless use of the automatic weapon. With the Thirty-sixth Division, the 442nd fought two more major battles for tiny towns before reaching the edge of the Vosges. Their orders were to push through the thick-timbered hills and valleys and to link up with General George Patton's Third Army for a final drive into Germany.

The Allied invasion of Sicily, July 1943

Then, abruptly, the Germans struck back. They quickly surrounded the First Battalion of the Thirty-sixth's 141st 'Alamo' Regiment, completely isolating it on a forbidding hilltop, Hill 645, known locally as Trapin des Saules, 'The Willows'. The regiment's two other battalions unsuccessfully attempted to break through and relieve their comrades. The 'Lost Battalion', as it came to be known, had been cut off for sixteen hours when, at 3 am on 27 October, the 442nd, the closest unit, was called to the rescue.

A JOB FOR SUPERMAN

It was a job for Superman, the soldiers were to joke later. Tersely, the 442nd was ordered to 'break though the reinforced German resistance' and 'relieve the First Battalion'. In the darkness they were to advance 8 kilometres through rough terrain, while the Lost Battalion tried to hold off further encirclement despite limited ammunition. The Germans had built a roadblock bristling with automatic weapons in the rescuers' path, and had defeated repeated efforts by the trapped unit to break through it.

The three battalions of the 442nd went forwards and engaged in heavy fighting. After twenty-four hours of bitter struggle, however, they were still 3 kilometres from the Lost Battalion, and rain was coming down in sheets. A new plan was now developed. The Germans were strongly established on a hill overlooking the site of the Lost Battalion, where they could pour down artillery barrages on the American positions. Sakato and the men of the Second Battalion were to hook around behind the Germans and attack from the rear while the other two battalions, backed by artillery and mortar fire, would hammer the enemy from the front.

One flanking company was driven back, but that was enough distraction for Sakato and E Company to advance—and for Sakato's great moment of bravery that was to earn him a Congressional Medal of Honor. Facing the enemy across an open clearing, he

... Sakato suddenly stood up and exhorted the others into the banzai charge. The Germans had never seen anything like it and they fled.

dodged forwards from foxhole to foxhole, killing five German soldiers and capturing four more. Then, as he stopped to reload, the platoon was pinned down by mortar and machine-gun fire. As his best friend Saburo Tanamachi died before his eyes, Sakato suddenly stood up and exhorted the others into the banzai charge. The Germans had never seen anything like it and they fled.

By early afternoon, the 442nd's Second Battalion had knocked the Germans off the hilltop. The Germans had lost 110 dead and 42 captured; the attackers eight dead and ten wounded. Sakato had killed twelve, wounded two, captured four and helped capture thirty-four others.

Meanwhile, the other two battalions fought a savage battle for possession of a fortified ridge grimly called 'Suicide Hill', which stood between the 442nd and the Lost Battalion. They staged another banzai charge, this time with bayonets. By nightfall, the whole hilly terrain was in 442 hands. Next morning, after another fierce firefight, in which Sakato was wounded, three men of the 442nd stepped across a clearing to greet three others in American uniforms. After eight days, the Lost Battalion had been saved. The battalion commander radioed headquarters: 'Patrol 442 [is] here. Tell them we love them'. To achieve the rescue, however, the 442nd had suffered 800 casualties—nearly four times the 212 rescued.

Ten days later, following heated debate in the Congress and Supreme Court about the violation of the rights of Japanese-Americans, Roosevelt announced that America's relocation camps would be closed and the residents would be free. The news about their families reached the 442nd just as they were being sent back to Italy to help finish up the job they had started earlier. Eventually, the 442 would become the most decorated unit of its size in U.S. military history, receiving an unprecedented 7 Presidential Unit Citations and 18,143 individual decorations, including 22 Congressional Medals of Honor and 9486 Purple Hearts.

A Last Bid For Glory

The Plot to Prevent Japan's Surrender

In July 1945, the leaders of the Allies met at Potsdam, Germany. On 16 July, the United States had successfully detonated its first test atomic device. Incendiary bombs had already left Tokyo's wooden buildings a charred ruin, and the country was starving. The Allies—now represented by Clement Attlee, replacing Churchill, and Harry Truman, who had succeeded Roosevelt, as well as Stalin—drew up what became known as the Potsdam Declaration, setting out stiff surrender terms for Japan, but making no mention of whether Emperor Hirohito would retain his position.

Confronting the terms, the Japanese leadership divided on whether to accept or reject the declaration. The 'Big Six' war council—consisting of the prime minister, foreign minister, war minister, navy minister and army and navy chiefs of staff—split evenly. While they were dithering, the first atomic bomb destroyed Hiroshima on 6 August. Truman warned that more devastation would follow unless the Japanese capitulated. More debate ensued and the second atomic bomb fell on Nagasaki on 9 August. Then the emperor broke the deadlock by making an unheard-of appearance before the cabinet to endorse the idea of a surrender.

THE PALE PROTÉGÉ

Surrender? Never, Major Kenji Hatanaka of the Imperial Army told himself. No matter that the emperor himself had said so. The enemy must not be permitted to enter the Japanese homeland; one hundred million Japanese had to be prepared to die first. No part of that honourable land should be yielded. Above all, no enemy hand should touch the emperor, who was to remain on his divine throne. The plan for surrender had to be stopped. The Big Six had to be thwarted and replaced. The war had to go on and the emperor had to be protected.

Hatanaka was a pale, thin-faced young officer in the military-affairs section headed by the war minister, General Korechika Anami, the most powerful man in the government. He was seen as Anami's pet and protégé, treated almost like a son. Hatanaka and a close colleague in the section, Lieutenant Colonel Masataka Ida, had together attended discussion groups that preached that it was the officers' sworn duty to serve and uphold the emperor unquestionably until death. There had already been talk at a higher level of a coup d'état, but it had evaporated. However, the two men convinced each other that the emperor had been

Japanese representatives arriving on board the USS *Missouri* to formally surrender to the Allies wrongly influenced and misled by a cabal of timorous officers. If these cowards could be removed, the emperor could be prevailed upon to change his decision.

On the evening of 11 August 1945, after a second Allied surrender demand, an excited Hatanaka, Ida and thirteen other officers attended a meeting in an underground bunker below the war ministry. Colonel Masahiko Takeshita, General Anami's brother-in-law, presided. The peace terms must be rejected and the surrender movement squelched, the group demanded. They must seize the Imperial Palace and dispose of the 'peace' faction. Takeshita was confident his brother-in-law would support them: 'I can guarantee that the general will join us'. Anami's chief of staff, General Yoshijiro Umezu, would then fall in line, as would the commanders of the two Tokyo garrisons, General Seiichi Tanaka of the Army's Eastern District and General Takeshi Mori of the Imperial Guard. This top-level cascade would continue down through the army. But it must all be accomplished quickly. Another Allied message was expected shortly. The conspirators had to strike before midnight on 13 August.

On 12 August, an Allied response was received. It repeated emphatically that the emperor would be subject to the authority of the Allied Supreme Commander, that he himself must agree to the Potsdam Declaration, and that the ultimate form of government would be determined by the 'will of the people'. It neither called for the removal of the emperor nor specifically left him in place. As soon as it was translated and its contents circulated, Hatanaka and the other conspirators went to chief of staff Umezu and demanded that he reject the contents of the note. Another group of young rebels went to the navy chief of staff, Admiral Soemu Toyoda, with the same demand. The two chiefs then called on the emperor and urged him to change his stance. Hirohito listened patiently and thanked them without committing himself.

The prime minister and the emperor's chief adviser would be imprisoned and the emperor placed in protective custody.

HERE'S OUR PLAN

Hatanaka spent that morning trying to reach Anami, certain he could win over his mentor to the rebels' cause. The war minister had been in and out of extended cabinet meetings to discuss the proposed surrender. Like the Big Six, the full cabinet split. There were three unacceptable sticking points to the Allied proposals, the opponents said. The emperor's sovereignty must be preserved, the Japanese islands must not be occupied and the form of government must not violate Japanese imperial tradition. Unless these conditions were met, the Japanese should go on fighting. The cabinet meeting ended in a stalemate.

The lack of support only inflamed the conspirators more. At 8 pm, ten of them confronted Anami at the war minister's official residence. They were led by Hatanaka and included Takeshita. Hatanaka arrived with a rumour he had picked up: the 'peace' faction planned to kill Anami the following morning if he did not support acceptance of the surrender terms. Anami scoffed. He was fifty-seven, an old warrior, he said, and did not fear death. At Takeshita's urging, Colonel Okikatsu Arao, senior officer of the military affairs section, then came forward with a piece of paper. 'Read it', said Anami and then listened.

The note outlined the coup that Hatanaka and his followers were planning. The rebellion was set for ten o'clock the next morning. General Mori had been approached and had promised to think about joining. His officers were all in favour of the coup. The prime minister and the emperor's chief adviser would be imprisoned and the emperor placed in protective custody. General Tanaka of the Eastern District would be asked to participate as soon as Anami consented to join.

Anami pussyfooted. 'Are you sure you've thought of everything?' he asked. 'Your groundwork seems a little vague. The plan is very incomplete.' But he said neither yes nor no; he refused to be pinned down, to stop the rebels or give them a go-ahead. When Hatanaka pleaded for a firm answer, Anami ushered the group out, still confused.

At 7 am on 14 August, with the 10 am deadline for the coup fast approaching, the conspirators accosted Anami once more. Anami's first move was to go to Umezu's office, accompanied by Arao. Point blank, he asked his chief of staff, 'Would you back a coup?' Umezu's answer was gruff and succinct. 'Absolutely not', he snapped. 'There is no chance of it succeeding. The people won't follow you.' Anami and Arao left, convinced the coup was finished.

THE EMPEROR'S PLEA

Tokyo was full of rumours, and some reached the emperor's ears. At 10 am on 14 August, he took an unusual step, calling a cabinet meeting for 10.30. With cabinet ministers scrambling for chairs, he listened quietly as the prime minister, the navy chief, Anami and Umezu detailed their views. Then the emperor declared in a soft, trembling voice, 'If there are no further views to present, I will present mine. I would like to have all of you agree with me. My view is still unchanged from that which I expressed at the conference on the ninth'—a reiteration, in other words, of his request that the government accept the Potsdam Declaration. Choking back tears, he continued,

> I cannot endure the thought of letting my people suffer any longer … It is my desire that you, my ministers of state, accede to my wishes and forthwith accept the Allied reply. In order that the people may know of my decision, I request you to prepare at once an Imperial rescript so that I may broadcast to the nation.

After he left the room, the cabinet routinely ratified his decision. The news spread rapidly and inspired the plotters to try once more to seize power. Takeshita went to Anami and again sought his support. 'No', the war minister said. 'It is too late.' He called together his staff and leadership, including Hatanaka and the other rebellious young officers. 'His Majesty has rendered his final decision in favour of terminating the war', he said. 'The Imperial Army must act in complete accord with this decision.'

Hatanaka burst into tears and fled from the room. He was determined that the coup would go on, with or without Anami, and regardless of the emperor's words. He jumped on his bicycle and pedalled furiously to the Eastern District headquarters, bursting in on General Seiichi Tanaka, the commanding general. Terminating the war, he exclaimed passionately, was 'a decision we cannot accept'. He urged Tanaka to station troops inside the palace, sever communications with the outside world and persuade the emperor to 'retrieve the situation'. Once that succeeded, he was sure the rest of the army would rise up and join. Attempting to win Tanaka over, he said untruthfully that he had already lined up General Mori of the Imperial Guard. Tanaka exploded. 'Go back to your barracks and stop this ridiculous scheme', he shouted. 'Do what you're told and accept what your leaders say. The war is over.'

Emperor Hirohito of Japan

Hatanaka didn't think it was over. He and his fellow plotters envisioned a military takeover that would keep the emperor on his throne. The armies would meet any Allied invasion and fight to the death before yielding a single centimetre of the homeland. The atomic bombs he simply disregarded. Lives had already been lost. What was more death and destruction in the face of such a noble cause?

Angrily, Hatanaka stormed out. Having already sounded out the leaders of the Imperial Palace Guard, he felt sure they would stand with him. Rounding up his friend Colonel Ida and two other young rebels, Captain Shigetaro Uehara of the air force and Lieutenant Colonel Jiro Shiizaki, he confronted Mori. Ida, the oldest and closest to Mori, described to the general the plans for the palace takeover and the expected army uprising. For more than an hour, Mori parried them with rambling tales of his own experiences and diversionary questions, playing for time while Hatanaka grew edgy and fingered his revolver. Losing patience, Hatanaka rushed out and appealed again to Takeshita, gaining a promise that Takeshita would try again to influence Anami.

Encouraged, Hatanaka hurried back to find Mori's rambling discourse still going on. When Ida briefly left the room, Hatanaka asked Mori for a frank yes-or-no answer. Mori tried to avoid the question again. Hatanaka snatched his pistol from its holster and shot him through the heart. As he fell, Uehara, or possibly Shiizaki, struck him with a sword on his left collarbone. Mori's aide rushed to his side. The antagonist swung the sword again and decapitated the aide. Hearing the commotion, Ida rushed back in. 'I had no time to argue, so I killed him', Hatanaka told him, business-like. Then, using Mori's official stamp, he forged orders for the First Regiment of Guards to move into the palace grounds, disarm the police and seal the compound.

HUNTING IN A SACRED DOMAIN

Hatanaka had learned that the emperor was to announce the surrender by radio at noon next day. A live appearance was considered beneath the emperor's station—indeed, the Japanese people had never before heard his voice—so the message had been recorded by the national radio NHK. Hatanaka realised he must destroy the recording before the broadcast. He rushed to the palace where the NHK technicians were still gathering up their equipment. He arrested them, hoping to learn the whereabouts of the recording. The NHK men disclosed that the record had been given to the court chamberlain, Yoshihiro Tokugawa. Unbeknownst to Hatanaka, Tokugawa had heard the conspirators and hidden himself in the palace's underground air-raid shelter.

Meanwhile, an air-raid alert was sounded and the palace lights were doused. Flashlight beams then stabbed through the darkness as Hatanaka and the others stumbled through the palace's labyrinthine corridors searching for the recording. Finally, at 4.30 am, they located the chamberlain, who angrily dressed them down for trespassing on the emperor's sacred domain. Even after being subjected to a punch in the face and a half hour of questioning, he professed ignorance of where the recording was hidden. (He had first stored it in the palace safe, then transferred it to a bin full of soiled bedsheets.)

Hatanaka's coup was collapsing, but he had one last card to play. Accompanied by a group of armed men, he invaded the NHK broadcasting studios. Waving his pistol at the announcer on duty, Morio Tateno, he demanded to be allowed to address the nation on the 5 am news broadcast. Tateno declined; because of the air-raid alert, no one could go on the air without army permission.

At that moment, the phone rang. It was Tanaka, who had traced Hatanaka to the radio station. Hatanaka listened, then said into the phone, 'I only want five minutes to let the nation know what the young officers think'. Permission was denied. Hatanaka turned to his entourage and said, 'We did our best. Let's go back to the palace'. He made one last feeble effort to win support for his views, distributing handbills to scornful passersby outside the palace. Then he slipped into a nearby copse of pines, put his pistol between his eyes and shot himself. A few hours later, the emperor's broadcast made Japan's surrender to the Allies official.

... the emperor was to announce the surrender by radio at noon next day. A live appearance was considered beneath the emperor's station ...

PART TWO

Stories of Tactics, Sieges, Survival and Escape

Thousands of Allied troops gather on the beach at Dunkirk during the massive evacaution in May 1940

Bridge To a War

The Conflict Begins in the East

I t hardly seemed the place or time for an incident that would spark an international conflagration. On the evening of 7 July 1937, Captain Frank Dorn, a U.S. assistant military attaché, watched with a smile as Western ladies and their escorts danced on the rooftop of the Hotel de Pekin, in China's former capital, Peking. The hotel was the social centre for diplomats and the international community. On warm nights, embassy personnel and business people gathered on the rooftop; in cooler weather, they descended to the ballroom. Peking reeked with foreign intrigue and diplomatic muscle-flexing, and increasing friction between Japan and China had caused some to predict outright war—indeed, one of the reasons Dorn and his boss, Colonel Joseph Stilwell, had been assigned to China was to keep an eye on Japan's military manoeuvring. But in the Hotel de Pekin on that night, it seemed most unlikely. 'War?' thought Dorn, 'What could be further away from this idyllic scene?'

Yet, at that moment, just out of earshot of the party guests, shots rang out in the dark—shots that would bring China into all-out war with Japan and lead to a sudden and dramatic widening of international conflict in the region. Some say they were the first shots, in the first battle, of World War II.

A BRIDGE WITH VERY FEW EQUALS

The shots came from the area of the Lugou Bridge over the Yongding River. The river separated Peking from the cities and agricultural plains to the south, where much of China's vast

Japanese troops
in Shanghai, 1937

population lived. The bridge had long been an important cultural and architectural landmark. Built in 1194, it consisted of eleven graceful granite arches supported by 281 pillars, each topped by a stone lion. Visiting in the thirteenth century, Marco Polo described it glowingly as 'a very fine stone bridge, so fine indeed that it has very few equals in the world'. Thereafter, it became known to Westerners as the Marco Polo Bridge. In 1937, the town of Wanping, at the east end of the bridge, was the site of one of four major Chinese military posts around central Peking.

Under an international treaty following the Boxer Rebellion, foreign nations were permitted to maintain garrisons in Peking, ostensibly to guard their embassies and to protect their citizens. Most garrisons consisted of small numbers of embassy guards. Japan, however, claiming ten thousand citizens in the Peking area, had a brigade of three infantry regiments, a tank group and a field-artillery regiment. Early on 7 July, the Japanese garrison had notified local authorities that its troops would conduct night field exercises on the western side of the bridge. As the exercises began, the Chinese guards at the bridge watched nervously, stiffened by a stern message from their commander: 'Under no circumstances permit an incident of any kind'.

> The history of recent Japanese-Chinese relations had been a series of such 'incidents', but this one seemed more menacing.

At 11 pm, the Japanese commander notified the Wanping garrison that a Japanese soldier was missing and that they believed him to be in the walled town, possibly being held captive. The commander demanded that the gates be opened so his troops could look for him. The Chinese leader refused, saying he must ask permission of his superiors. The Japanese commander gave him an hour. When the deadline passed at midnight, the Japanese began bombarding the town. At dawn, they attacked with a force of about three thousand infantry, backed by tanks. The Japanese were to claim later that the attack was self-defence—a response to a spray of gunfire from the town and the guards on the bridge.

The defenders, like much of the Chinese Kuomintang, or Nationalist, army, were armed only with their traditional broadswords, some antique rifles and a few mortars and machine guns. They had no weapons against tanks and were little match for the well-trained, well-equipped Japanese soldiers. By mid-morning on 8 July, the Japanese had overrun the Chinese and were a few metres from capturing the rail junction at Wanping leading to the major cities of Shanghai and Hankou. But then, reinforced by other army units hurriedly brought in, the Chinese struck back and recovered the bridge. At this point, the Japanese commander halted the battle and suggested negotiations.

A FIRST-HAND REPORT

Next morning, 9 July, with Japanese planes sweeping over the city and the occasional burst of rifle fire or mortar still being heard, Colonel Stilwell called Dorn and another attaché, Major David Barrett, to his office. Stilwell, known then and later as 'Vinegar Joe' for his acidulous and sarcastic speech, looked grim. Peking was full of reports and rumours about the Wanping incident. The Associated Press had reported erroneously that the Japanese attack had destroyed the treasured bridge. Washington was on the wire. America had a paternalistic relationship with China; generations of American missionaries had served in China and their voices were influential in China policy. Stilwell wanted facts about the stand-off, not unfounded stories. He told Dorn and Barrett to take the staff car and drive to the bridge for a first-hand report.

Dorn was a West Pointer with an artistic bent (he was later to design the shoulder patch for U.S. armies in the China-Burma-India theatre and exhibit prize-winning paintings) and had spent four years in the Philippines and learned Chinese from the local community. He (like Stilwell) could communicate with the Chinese military in their own language. Even so, when Dorn and Barrett reached Wanping, the gates were closed and weren't being opened for anybody. Instead, they watched as the Chinese commander atop the town wall shouted angrily at the Japanese officer below. The Japanese led the Americans to a spot where, they said, the crumpled body of the 'missing' man had been found, and had another soldier pose in the 'dead' man's position.

The attachés noted the presence of Japanese artillery and large numbers of troops, far more than would have been needed for a search. Clearly, the Japanese meant to stay. When the attachés reported back to Stilwell, he looked grimmer yet. The history of recent Japanese-Chinese relations had been a series of such 'incidents', but this one seemed more menacing. Stilwell began to suspect a major confrontation was on the cards.

OVER THE GREAT WALL

Japan had been biting off bits of northern China for almost a decade. Industrialised Japan needed raw materials and had few resources at home. In 1931, it had seized China's resource-rich province of Manchuria, renaming it Manchukuo and establishing a puppet government. The next year, Japanese forces surmounted China's ancient Great Wall, and occupied part of the central province of Hubei. The Japanese claimed, with some justification, that the occupations were necessary to protect Manchuria against bandits and brigands, as well as the Soviet Communist regime.

The combination of Japanese muscle-flexing and territorial and economic takeovers had aroused strong anti-Japanese feeling among politicians and population alike. Belligerent warlords and the Chinese Communist party, headed by Mao Zedong and Zhou Enlai, protested the Japanese presence and pressed the shaky Chinese leader, Chiang Kai-shek, to oppose it. Chiang delayed action until the frustrated opposition kidnapped him from his bed on 12 December 1936, whisking him away so quickly that he even left behind his false teeth. He was released (and reunited with his false teeth) only when he agreed to join the warlords and the Communists in a united front against the Japanese, and assign a division of his Nationalist troops to the Marco Polo Bridge.

'THESE FLARE-UPS COME AND GO'

Like Stilwell, Dorn took the bridge incident seriously, but few others in Peking did. Once it was clear that the beloved bridge was largely unscathed, Peking went back to its business and social whirl. When Dorn tried to convince some of the city's 2000 Americans that they should perhaps take refuge in the coastal cities or head home, he was laughed at. 'Young man', an American woman missionary in Peking told him, 'when you've been here as long as I have, you'll realise these flare-ups come and go. They always have. But the voice of God is heard above them all.'

But when the Japanese and Chinese negotiators met two weeks after the incident, the tone was hardly conciliatory. The Chinese were unexpectedly presented with a take-it-or-leave-it ultimatum. The Japanese would agree not to attack Peking or Tientsin, another important northern Chinese city, on three conditions: Chiang's Kuomintang must close down all anti-Japanese organisations and halt all anti-Japanese activities; it must also take all responsibility for initiating the 7 July bridge incident and punish those responsible; and the commanding general of the Chinese army, Song Zheyuan, must apologise—no mere underling would do.

The negotiator accepted the first two conditions—the field commander at the bridge had already been transferred elsewhere—but noted that he could not answer for General Song nor give an apology; he would have to consult with his superiors. He had scarcely returned to his headquarters when the Japanese attacked. Chiang, backed by the warlords and Communists, turned any further negotiations down. After a fierce bombardment, Japanese

The combination of Japanese muscle-flexing and territorial and economic takeovers had aroused strong anti-Japanese feeling among politicians and population alike.

troops stormed into Peking's Forbidden City on 28 July and took Tientsin two days later. The Flag of the Rising Sun now flew over all of northern China, and the North China Plain and central China lay open to the Japanese.

After another incident, in which a Japanese officer killed a Chinese sentry at Shanghai on 9 August 1937, before being killed himself, Japan moved an entire army into that port city on 11 August, along with a naval force of battleships and carriers. Three months of street fighting ended with a Nationalist defeat. In December 1937, Japanese armies ravaged the national capital of Nanjing. By then, Chinese and Japanese were fighting across the entire littoral. Stilwell's fears had come to pass. Moreover, by then another international dimension had been added, Italy having joined Japan and Germany in the Anti-Comintern Pact. The Rome-Berlin-Tokyo Axis was now forged.

THE *PANAY* AFFAIR

Dorn was sent to both Shanghai and Nanjing to observe, and fed alarming reports of Japanese atrocities and Chinese military ineptitude to Stilwell. In December 1937, the United States sent a gunboat, the *Panay*, up the Yangtze to evacuate Americans from Nanjing. Although the *Panay* was clearly marked with an American flag, it was attacked by Japanese dive-bombers. Its captain was severely wounded and three sailors killed. As the ship sank, planes strafed the survivors as they tried to reach shore. Hours later, a British gunboat, the *Ladybird*, was also attacked.

Although the Japanese immediately apologised, U.S. naval intelligence decoded a message indicating that the attack had been planned by senior officers aboard a nearby Japanese carrier. The reports inflamed the American public and Washington, which sent an additional detachment of marines to China, and began a 'preparedness' arms build-up. The British sent two battleships to the Pacific and strengthened their garrison at Singapore. Both countries now saw Japan as a major threat to world peace and began preparing for a possible showdown.

In July 1938, the Japanese picked another fight along the Manchurian–Siberian–Korean border, where a number of incidents had already occurred. They moved in on a steep height, clearly in Soviet territory, from where they could survey the border. But they ran into a well-dug-in force of Soviet troops backed by aircraft, and after a month were forced to withdraw ignominiously.

The next year, on 11 May, they tried again in another area. At first, they were successful in capturing several parcels of Soviet territory. But on 20 August, General Georgy Zhukov, later the hero of Stalingrad, arrived with 350 tanks, 340 armoured cars, artillery, combat aircraft and four divisions of infantry. Full-scale combat involving 150,000 troops ensued, and in five days the Japanese were knocked back, and agreed to a ceasefire.

WHO FIRED THE FIRST SHOT?

A chain of events had been set off that would lead Japan to war with not only China and Russia, but all of the Allied Powers. For seasoned observers like Frank Dorn, it could all be traced back to that July night on the Marco Polo Bridge. But mystery still shrouded the exact cause of the incident that came to be seen by many as the first battle of World War II. Who had actually fired the first shots at the bridge?

Even today, this is still debated. One explanation is that a jittery Chinese or Japanese recruit fired his gun accidentally, setting off a cascade of fire. A more widely accepted version is that the 'missing soldier' story was a hoax, perpetrated by the Japanese to allow them to extend their domain into central China. After all, no soldier was ever found—and it certainly seemed odd that the Japanese could overnight summon a large force just to look for a lost private.

Sneaking Into The British Lair

The Surprise German Attack on Scapa Flow

The war in Europe was scarcely a month old when Admiral Karl Dönitz, submarine commander of the German navy, summoned Lieutenant Commander Günther Prien to his Kiel headquarters. The ramrod-straight Prien, barely thirty-one, and the crew of his submarine *U-47* had been credited with sinking three Britain-bound merchant vessels in the Atlantic, and Prien had already won his first Iron Cross. Prien entered Dönitz's office and saluted smartly. The commander waved him to a chair. Then he began to tell the young officer about something that had been eating away at him for twenty years.

In World War I, the young Dönitz had commanded a U-boat that had been attacked and sunk, and he and his crew had been taken prisoner until 1920. At the Armistice, the German High Seas Fleet had surrendered and its vessels had been impounded at the British naval stronghold of Scapa Flow in Scotland's Orkney Islands. In the summer of 1919, while most of the British fleet was at sea, the German commander had ordered the German fleet scuttled. Fifty-nine capital ships were either heavily damaged or sunk. On learning of the scuttling, prisoner Dönitz had been outraged. Those ships could have been the nucleus of a revived post-war fleet. It was an inglorious end for the gallant fleet. Now war had erupted again, Dönitz wanted revenge. What he had in mind was a submarine attack on Scapa Flow, with Prien in command.

Part of the British fleet at anchor in Scapa Flow in the Orkney Islands, Scotland

Dönitz had another agenda, too. The navy commander in chief, Admiral Ernst Raeder, and the rest of the naval leadership believed that surface raiders, like the fast 'pocket battleships' *Deutschland* (soon renamed the *Lützow* because Hitler did not want to risk the sinking of a ship named after the fatherland) and *Admiral Graf Spee*, were the key to harassing the merchant shipping on which Britain depended. According to this viewpoint, submarines were valuable, but battleships were more manoeuvrable and carried far more firepower. Indeed, *Deutschland* and *Graf Spee* were already ranging the oceans and giving the mighty British fleet fits. Dönitz, on the contrary, thought that undersea craft were Germany's ultimate seaborne offensive weapon. In his opinion, they were superior in that they could go anywhere unseen and cut loose on unsuspecting enemies with devastating torpedoes. For Dönitz, no enemy vessel was safe from submarines, nor was any enemy haven secure—and he aimed to prove it. All that was needed was a major strike on a supposedly secure enemy bastion. Prien, with his proven ingenuity, seamanship and bravery, was the man for the job. And Scapa Flow was the ideal target.

A waterway amid the Orkney Islands north of Scotland, Scapa Flow was the home anchorage for Britain's great fleet of battleships and battle cruisers, and was considered invulnerable to submarine attack. The tides and currents that raged around the islands ranged from fierce to devastating. There were limited entrances and channels to the Flow, and the British had sown them with all manner of underwater hazards: blockships weighted down by concrete, heavy cables and nets stretched from shore to shore and gates that could be raised or lowered to thwart entry. As Dönitz explained to Prien, there had been two unsuccessful attempts

MEANWHILE, ON THE SURFACE . . .

By early October 1939, the raider *Admiral Graf Spee* had already accounted for nine merchant ships sunk in the South Atlantic. The British Admiralty decided the nine-thousand-tonne 'pocket battleship' must be tracked down and destroyed. As the *U-47* set out on its fateful voyage, the Royal Navy assembled eight hunting groups to pursue the *Graf Spee* in the South Atlantic and Indian oceans. Much of the Scapa Flow anchorage emptied as the hunters put to sea. Unfortunately, because of radio silence, Dönitz could not notify Prien that his quarry had flown.

It was not until 13 December that Hunting Group G, consisting of the heavy cruiser *Exeter*, the light cruiser *Ajax* and the cruiser *Achilles* of the Royal New Zealand Navy, caught up with the *Graf Spee* off the coast of Uruguay. The battle of the River Plate ensued. The *Exeter* was heavily damaged, but the *Graf Spee* was crippled by a hit in the boiler room. It went into the neutral port of Montevideo but could not make repairs. Forced by international law to leave after three days, the captain ordered the pride of the German fleet scuttled, then shot himself dead.

by German submarines to enter Scapa Flow during World War I. Both subs had been detected and sunk.

So, would Lieutenant Commander Prien be willing to undertake such a daring and dangerous mission? Dönitz didn't need an immediate answer. He gave Prien an armload of charts, topographic maps, tide tables and climate observations, plus another armload of recent Luftwaffe reconnaissance photos, and told him, 'Go home and study these and report back with your decision in forty-eight hours'. Prien returned next day with another smart salute and an affirmative answer. Dönitz shook the young man's hand. 'Get your boat ready', he said.

SECRECY AND SECRET WEAPONS

The noted American radio reporter and historian William L. Shirer, in his broadcasts and in his book *Berlin Diary*, described Prien on first meeting as 'clean-cut, cocky, a fanatical Nazi and obviously capable'. At twenty-three, following several years on merchant ships, Prien had enlisted in the navy. After serving as an officer on the light cruiser *Königsberg*, he transferred to the submarine services after the Nazis came to power and began building up the fleet. He rose rapidly and received his first command, the *U-47*, a few months before the war broke out. In its initial North Atlantic patrol, the *U-47* destroyed 60,000 tonnes of British shipping.

Dönitz christened his dream raid 'Operation Order North Sea Number 16'. He scheduled it for midnight of 13–14 October. There would be no moon and the Scapa Flow tide would be full, the better to navigate over the shallower depths. The *U-47* was to travel with explosives already rigged so that it could be scuttled at a moment's notice if capture seemed imminent. It was to be stripped of all secret papers and nonessential equipment, such as the Enigma code machine used to decipher coded messages (see page 74), lest the sub fall into enemy hands. And it was

For Dönitz, no enemy vessel was safe from submarines, nor was any enemy haven secure—and he aimed to prove it.

to scrap its steam-driven torpedoes in favour of the submarine service's newest, most secret weapon, the electric-powered G7e torpedo, which left no wake that could be traced back to the firing vessel. The British had no idea such a weapon existed.

Utmost secrecy was essential. Even Prien's forty-four-man crew, mostly energetic eighteen- and nineteen-year-olds, was not told the destination nor the objectives of the mission. No orders or papers were drawn up; Dönitz even briefed Raeder face to face, leaving no paper trail. All German vessels in the vicinity of the Orkneys were to be withdrawn until the mission succeeded—or failed.

ON TO SCAPA FLOW

Just after sunrise on Sunday 8 October 1939, the *U-47* slipped quietly out of the Kiel base and headed towards the North Sea. For the next four days, the ship crept towards its target. To the puzzlement of the crew, the sub moved only at night; if another ship appeared, even an inviting target, the normally combative captain gave the order to immediately submerge and hide. During the day, the *U-47* remained on the seabed. Finally, when the sub was only some two nautical miles off the Scottish coast, Prien called the crew together and revealed the secret plan. He told his men that they would enter Scapa Flow the next day. Theirs would be a hazardous mission, one of great risks, from which they might not return. But, if successful, it would strike a mighty blow—a triumphant blow—for the Fatherland.

That afternoon, after what they referred to as 'our last supper', the men readied the *U-47*, checking the torpedoes and the scuttling charges. Beginning at 7.15 pm the ship rose to the surface. Prien ascended the conning tower, and was astonished by what he saw. On what was supposed to be a moonless night, the sky was filled with light. Blazing across the sky, the northern lights reflected off the vessel's surface, making the *U-47* plain to see.

> Utmost secrecy was essential. Even Prien's forty-four-man crew, mostly energetic eighteen- and nineteen-year-olds, was not told the destination nor the objectives of the mission.

What should he do? Prien first concluded that he might have to carry out the mission submerged, despite Dönitz's orders. Then he reconsidered. The *U-47* began to edge slowly towards the easternmost entry to Scapa Flow. When a lookout spotted a merchant ship approaching, Prien gave the order to dive. But once under water, peering through his periscope, he couldn't see the merchantman clearly. That meant he would have trouble seeing his target, and he couldn't risk that. A surface attack clearly would be necessary if the mission were to succeed.

Surfacing again, he headed into the Flow without being challenged and steered for a fifteen-metre gap between two blockships. He first had to cross heavy wire cables, thirty centimetres thick, which held the blockships in place. The *U-47* scraped the cables with a rasping jolt that shook the vessel then pushed it to one side, running it aground. Despite Prien's best efforts with engine and rudder, the submarine would not budge.

It appeared that the expedition could end ignominiously, with the would-be attacker stranded in the sand, like a beached whale. Prien had visions of himself and his crew captured and paraded through British streets as prisoners of war. But then something came to mind. Prien had originally ordered the sub's ballast tanks flooded to lower its silhouette in the water; now, in desperation, he ordered the tanks to be emptied. And as the *U-47* floated free, he breathed a huge sigh of relief.

Now in the inner reaches of the Flow, Prien cruised westwards for six kilometres, expecting at any moment to spot the powerful British Home Fleet, its battleships lined up hull to hull. But none appeared. He reversed course and headed back towards the entry point. Still nothing, just a few empty docks and piers. To Prien's bitter disappointment, it seemed that their dangerous hunt had been a wild goose chase. The Home Fleet was nowhere to be seen.

A frustrated Prien decided to have one last look before tides and current turned against him. He spun to explore the northeastern corner of the anchorage. There, at last, he discerned the huge, dim but unmistakable silhouette of a British battleship, which he correctly assumed to be the *Royal Oak*. Beyond he could see a second ship, partly hidden, which he took to be a battle cruiser, mistakenly identifying it as the *Repulse*. Still on the surface, the *U-47* moved to within 3,200 metres. The excited crew prepared the four forward torpedo tubes. Two were trained on the *Royal Oak*, the other two took aim at the more distant target.

KNOCKED FROM THEIR BEDS

It was nearly 1 am and the 1,200-man *Royal Oak* crew was mostly asleep. The twenty-six-thousand-tonne vessel, a veteran of World War I, had been left behind while other ships sailed off to pursue the German surface raiders—with a top speed of only twenty knots, *Royal Oak* was deemed too slow to keep pace with the newer vessels. It was scheduled to move to a new posting next day, so the men were having a last rest in port.

Suddenly they were startled from their bunks by a small explosion amidships. Running to investigate, they discovered water cascading over the forward deck. The ship's captain, William Benn, was told the cause was a minor internal explosion, probably something in the refrigeration mechanism. All returned to bed.

In fact, the *U-47* had fired three torpedoes; a fourth jammed in its tube. One of the torpedoes that had fired had caused the small explosion, but the other two had either missed or misfired. Prien disgustedly blamed faulty torpedoes and wheeled to fire the stern torpedo. That missed, too. He cursed.

He had been assigned an important mission and could not possibly turn tail, not with the quarry within his sights. He ordered the bow tubes reloaded and the jammed tube cleared for refiring. He moved the sub closer and fired from all three tubes. Within ten seconds, the torpedoes tore three holes amidships on the starboard side of the *Royal Oak*. The blasts set off fires that enveloped the magazine. Tonnes of ammunition exploded with a roar, ripping through the decks. With water pouring in through the holes below the waterline, the battleship listed forty-five degrees to starboard. Its heavy guns weighted it down; half-tonne shells rolled off their racks, one after another, adding to the lopsidedness and shaking the ship. Men scrambled to escape through the port side. Just thirteen minutes after the first hit the *Royal Oak*, once the pride of the fleet, turned over and dropped beneath the waves. Eight hundred and thirty-three men went to their deaths with her. One was Rear Admiral Henry Blagrove, commander of the Second Battle Squadron.

Admiral Dönitz greeting Prien after the mission

Watching the horrific scene through binoculars from the *U-47* conning tower, Prien saw the *Royal Oak* slip beneath the surface. He turned to his crew with satisfaction. 'She's finished', he said and gave the order to move out at full speed. Successfully navigating between the blockships and cables, and despite fighting a ten-knot current, the *U-47* threaded its way out of Scapa Flow and in forty-five minutes was back in the North Sea. 'We are going home', he told the cheering crew.

On shore, everything was in chaos. Searchlights swept the sky, anti-aircraft batteries aimed upwards seeking a target, RAF pilots scrambled to their planes. Commanders were convinced a German bomber, undetected by British defences, was responsible for the attack—a plane had in fact been seen overflying the base a few days before. The attacker couldn't have been a submarine, they said. Everyone knew that no German U-boat could penetrate the nets, ropes, tricky currents and capricious tides that protected invulnerable Scapa Flow. A week later, however, divers sifting the wreckage for bodies stumbled onto the propeller of a German torpedo. The Admiralty assured the public that Scapa Flow was safe and that the intrusive sub had been sunk.

Eight hundred and thirty-three men went to their deaths with her.

It was not until 16 October, three days after the raid, that Prien broke radio silence and informed Dönitz of his spectacular success. Hailed as a conqueror, the young commander was personally decorated by Hitler and became known as 'a hero of heroes' and 'The Bull of Scapa Flow'. Wearing yet another Iron Cross, he rejoined Dönitz's submarine 'wolfpacks' to prey on Allied convoys, picking off shipload after valuable shipload along the North American coast. By the time the *U-47* was sunk, apparently by a British destroyer, on 8 March 1941, it had claimed thirty merchantmen, a total of about 150,000 tonnes of Allied shipping.

How To Make a Molotov Cocktail

Russia's Disastrous Invasion of Finland

It was a simple concoction, really. Devised during the Spanish Civil War, the 'cocktail' required the nearest available glass bottle, which was then filled with petrol or another inflammable, explosive liquid. A petrol-soaked rag was twisted into the neck and lit, and the bottle was thrown at an inviting target, where it would explode on impact. With good aim—or luck—it would land on or near an enemy tank and bring the vehicle to a shuddering halt.

This makeshift missile was just one element of the nightmare that confronted the men of the invading Soviet armies at Suomussalmi, a logging town in the forests of Finland, in December 1939. It was not at all the kind of reception the Soviet troops had anticipated. They had been told they would be greeted as liberators, rescuers of the loggers and pulp-factory workers of this frigid, sparsely populated land from an oppressive capitalist regime. The Russians arrived with a brass band to announce their triumphant entry, a printing press, stacks of leaflets extolling the glories of life in an unshackled, working-class, Marxist state, and bags and bags of goodwill gifts. And they bristled with all the tools of modern warfare—tanks, heavy-duty artillery, machine guns, grenades and combat aircraft. Plus men—masses and masses of men, marching resolutely forwards along the narrow logging roads bordered by towering, thick forests that blotted out the meagre winter light. They outnumbered the Finnish forces five to one.

> A petrol-soaked rag was twisted into the neck and lit, and the bottle was thrown at an inviting target, where it would explode on impact.

Finnish ski troops mobilising
near the Russo-Finnish border
in October 1939

But the Soviets had to cope with temperatures thirty degrees below zero Celsius and inadequate equipment—many of the soldiers had come from the southern Soviet Union and were left shivering in lightweight uniforms, their leaders being so confident of a quick campaign that they had seen no need to issue winter gear. Moreover, they were also met with very determined opposition. The men of Finland may have lacked the numbers and many of the armaments of their opponents, but they boasted key weapons of their own: mobility, ingenuity, stubbornness and devotion to their homeland. And at Suomussalmi, these assets were augmented by another: the innovativeness of a short, blunt-spoken reserve officer, Lieutenant Colonel Hjalmar Siilasvuo.

Siilasvuo was to deal an embarrassing blow to the Soviet military machine that would reverberate through the early years of the war. Even today, the creative tactics of this Finnish village lawyer and the men who followed him are still taught at military academies the world over.

FINLAND'S GREAT HERO

Although they were of a different ethnic origin from the Russians, the Finns had been part of the czarist empire from Napoleonic times until 1918. Then, at the end of World War I, the Versailles Treaty, emphasising a people's right to self-determination, had established a self-governing, democratic Finland. This, however, triggered a civil war between the Finnish Red Guards, who sought to establish a Communist state, and the anti-Bolshevik White Guards. Though the Whites triumphed under an inspiring leader, Baron Carl Gustaf Mannerheim, the Finnish Communist Party remained strong in the sawmills and wood-pulp factories that were Finland's economic backbone.

Finland and Soviet Russia bordered each other in the region known as Karelia. In the south, they were linked by the Karelian

Isthmus, a narrow strip of land between the Gulf of Finland and Lake Ladoga. It was a historic approach route to Leningrad (known earlier, and today, as St Petersburg), Russia's second-largest city, one-time capital, cultural centre and cradle of the 1917 Bolshevik revolution. The Finnish border lay only thirty kilometres from the Leningrad outskirts. Peter the Great, the czar who established the city as Russia's window on the Baltic and to the West, had fretted, given the presence of his threatening neighbour Sweden, that 'the ladies of St Petersburg could not sleep comfortably with the border so close at hand'.

It made Stalin uneasy, too. Hence, early in 1939, he summoned the Finnish foreign minister to demand additional territory to protect Leningrad. He asked that the border be moved back another thirty kilometres—'Since we can't move Leningrad', he told the foreign minister jovially, 'we will have to move the border'. He also asked for a chunk of Karelia, which the two countries shared, four sparsely inhabited Finnish islands commanding the approaches to Leningrad, the rights to build a naval base on Finnish territory and a handover of the ice-free port of Petsamo on the Arctic Ocean. In return, the Finns would get some Karelian wastelands then in Soviet hands.

But the Finns were not about to give up their territory that easily. They yielded two of the four islands—no one lived there, anyway—and consented to the naval base. For the rest, they agreed to negotiate, and they did, for months, getting nowhere. On 9 November, the Soviet foreign minister, V.M. Molotov, snapped, saying, 'Since we civilians don't seem to be making any progress, perhaps it is the soldiers' turn to speak'. The first shots were fired on 26 November, and on 30 November Soviet troops crossed the border into Finland, claiming that they were defending a puppet Communist state just set up on Finnish territory.

The men of Finland may have lacked the numbers ... but they boasted key weapons of their own: mobility, ingenuity, stubbornness and devotion to their homeland.

NO PUSHOVER

As the Soviet leader Nikita Khrushchev was to write many years later, everyone in the Kremlin leadership in 1939 assumed the Finns would be a pushover. 'All we had to do was raise our voices a little bit, and the Finns would obey', Khrushchev said. 'If that didn't work, we could fire one shot and the Finns would put up their hands and surrender. Or so we thought.' The small country had only 130,000 troops, most of them reservists, supported by twelve antiquated aircraft and six tanks. The Finnish army had just received its first two antitank guns. The Soviets, by contrast, mustered four armies, an invasion force of five hundred thousand men, with 500 planes, 2,500 tanks and armoured cars, and 2,000 guns. The war would all be over quickly, the Soviets were sure.

The Soviets divided their forces and struck in several directions at once. The first strike was launched across the Karelian Isthmus and was designed to push the Finns back towards the putative new border. A second attack targeted Finnish positions in Karelia, and a third was to drive straight across Finland towards the vital port of Oulu on the Gulf of Bothnia, the shipping point for ores from the nickel and iron mines of Arctic Finland and Sweden. If the Soviets reached Oulu, Finland would be cut in half. Their main obstacle was Suomussalmi, a logging settlement of four thousand people and the junction point for roads and rail lines from the north and towards Oulu and Sweden.

When Hjalmar Siilasvuo was given command of regiment JR-27 of the Finnish Ninth Division at Suomussalmi, he immediately recognised an opportunity. With its tanks, armoured cars, mobile kitchens and trucks, the approaching Soviet 163rd Division of seventeen thousand was strictly confined to the narrow, winding and limited roads, where it was strung out for eight kilometres, with many gaps in the ranks. Siilasvuo's own troops, on the other hand, were outdoorsmen, who were familiar with the forests and

Finnish women and children flee during the Russian invasion of Finland

were able to move readily and easily through the trees. All had literally grown up on cross-country skis.

Consequently, Siilasvuo decided it was time to employ the *motti* tactic. A *motti* in Finnish is a staked enclosure in the forest where logs or timbers are stacked until ready to be chopped into firewood. Although the Soviets outnumbered the Finns, their force was stretched out along the road in formations of varying lengths. With no place to run but the forbidding woods, these formations were vulnerable—like the logs in a *motti*, ripe for cutting into smaller pieces. By concentrating his forces on one 'log' at a time, Siilasvuo obtained numerical superiority.

By 28 December, all Soviet resistance around Suomussalmi had ended, many of the Soviet soldiers fleeing across the frozen lake in, they hoped, the general direction of Russia.

Siilasvuo sent his ski troops into the forests at the head and tail of the Soviet unit that reconnaissance had shown to be the weakest. Clad head to foot in white uniforms that blended with the snow and concealed them amid the brooding forests, the Finns quickly surrounded the unsuspecting Soviets. They silently slipped out of their skis ('Never fight on your skis if you can avoid it', Siilasvuo and the Finnish high command preached), unlimbered their rifles and attacked, first firing from a prone position that made them indistinguishable from the snow, then closing in and fighting hand to hand until the Soviets fled or surrendered.

Siilasvuo then used a variation of the *motti* tactic against the remaining force. He ordered his troops to surround the units he regarded as too strong to be attacked and keep them pinned at the road. The Finns concentrated their fire on the mobile kitchens and the log fires the Soviets built to keep themselves warm, which silhouetted the Russian soldiers, making them easy prey. The chief enemies of the Soviets now, exactly as Siilasvuo had anticipated, were hunger and cold; further military action wasn't required. In a single day, figures showed later, one trapped Soviet regiment suffered 43 cases of frostbite and 160 more casualties due to exposure and hypothermia.

Siilasvuo then 'allowed' the Soviets to advance to their original destination, Suomussalmi, but the town had been put to the torch and offered no shelter. Some troops managed to cross the frozen arm of the lake on which the village was situated to another tiny town, Kylanmaki, but they were quickly surrounded and pinned down there, too.

QUICK! WHICH WAY TO RUSSIA?

On Christmas Day, 1939, Siilasvuo was reinforced with a full infantry regiment of 'ski guerillas', plus a more traditional infantry battalion, giving him a total of 11,500 men and a promotion to brigadier, and he squeezed the nutcracker. By 28 December, all Soviet resistance around Suomussalmi had ended, many of the Soviet soldiers fleeing across the frozen lake in, they hoped, the general direction of Russia. Easily spotted in their khaki uniforms against the bleak, white, frozen surface, they were cut down by Finnish machine-gunners. Soon, the Soviet 163rd Division had

I WANT TO FIGHT, TOO

When mighty Russia attacked in late 1939, sympathy for 'poor little Finland' arose worldwide. Would-be fighters from Britain, the United States and France volunteered to join the cause. Because the Winter War was so brief, few got the chance, but plenty were already fighting elsewhere. The Spanish Civil War had attracted volunteers from many countries, especially on the Loyalist (Republican) side, as famously described in George Orwell's *Homage to Catalonia* and Ernest Hemingway's *For Whom the Bell Tolls*. One famous unit, the Abraham Lincoln Brigade, made up mainly, but not exclusively, of young American Communists and sympathisers, fought valiantly in several key battles around Valencia and Madrid.

Before the US sided with the Allies, so many young American flyers went to Canada 'to get in on the war' that people joked that RCAF stood for 'Royal Californian Air Force'. Other American flyers went to China as the American Volunteer Group, to fight with the Nationalists in 1940 against the Japanese. Recruited by retired U.S. Colonel (later General) Clare Chennault, they became known as the 'Flying Tigers'.

ceased to exist. The Finns counted five thousand frozen bodies on the road, and no one could guess how many more might be found in the woods.

While the 163rd Division had been pinned down, another division, the Forty-fourth, had been sent to its rescue—too late, as it turned out, to do any good. This heavily mechanised division, considered one of the Soviet's best, also stayed to the roads. Siilasvuo had one of his battalion commanders build a manned roadblock in the division's path, across a narrow neck of land between two arms of the frozen lake. Then again he applied his *motti* tactics, picking off sections one by one, overwhelming some and leaving others to starve or freeze. He supplemented these tactics by lining the road with snipers, whom the Russians called 'cuckoos'. Wearing white, these ghostly figures would tie themselves to trees and wait patiently for an officer to come into sight before firing. They seldom missed. Unused to such tactics, the Soviets panicked. Every gunshot was answered with a wild barrage of firing. Soon, the Forty-fourth ran low on ammunition. Its commander, General Vinogradov, called for an air strike, but the planes, unable to spot anyone below in the dense forests, simply wasted their bombs. By early January, the division had run out of fuel, ammunition and food. Finally, it, too, broke apart and went out of existence. Vinogradov fled back to the Russian lines, where he was immediately court-martialled and shot.

MIXING A BETTER COCKTAIL

Along with their unorthodox tactics, the Finns relied heavily on unorthodox weapons, most notably their antitank 'cocktail', which they named the 'Molotov cocktail' in a derisive jab at the Soviet foreign minister. The Finns refined the original recipe, adding kerosene, motor oil and sugar to make the flaming liquid adhere to its target. To prevent the wick blowing out, they attached a

Bengal light to the side, which kept smouldering until the cocktail hit its mark. The Finns also refined the method of using the cocktail. Ski troopers would creep quietly up to the tanks at night and tuck a cocktail under the tank treads so that it would explode when the tank moved. Combined with the intense cold, which forced the Russians to keep their tanks running continuously so that they did not freeze, the cocktails helped neutralise the Soviet tank units.

Learning of Siilasvuo's success, Finnish armies up and down the country copied the *motti* tactic—the so-called 'Great Motti' in the Karelia annihilated an entire Soviet division. But as winter turned to spring, the continuous fighting weakened the Finnish forces and the warmer weather robbed them of their advantage. In March, with his forces dwindling, Mannerheim sued for peace. The Soviets took over the isthmus, the islands, the naval base and a great chunk of Karelia. Yet, looking at a map of their gains, one Russian general is reported to have said, 'We have won just about enough ground to bury our dead'. The official Russian losses, in what would come to be known as the Winter War, were 48,745 dead, but historians say the real total was 230,000 to 270,000 dead. The Finns lost about 25,000.

The Winter War helped torpedo the reputation of the Red Army as a mighty force. When Hitler launched his Operation Barbarossa offensive against the Soviet Union the following year, the U.S. Army chief of staff, General George Marshall, predicted to President Roosevelt that the Red Army would be soundly defeated within three months. Some British military experts gave the Soviets just sixty days. Meanwhile, the Finns joined the German offensive and played a major role in the climactic, nine-hundred-day siege of Leningrad—much as Stalin had feared.

The Finns counted five thousand frozen bodies on the road, and no one could guess how many more might be found in the woods.

Calling All Boats!

'The Miracle of Dunkirk'

Early on the morning of 28 May 1940, Douglas Tough was standing outside his boatyard in Teddington, west of London, watching the Thames River roll by peacefully. In the boatyard office, the BBC radio was solemnly delivering uncomfortable news about the fighting in France, less than two hundred kilometres away, but Tough paid little attention. Then the ringing of his telephone jarred him out of his reverie. It was a surprise, for people didn't usually phone that early.

Tough stepped inside, picked up the phone and heard an unfamiliar voice at the end of the line. The caller identified himself as Admiral Sir Lionel Preston, director of something called the Small Vessels Pool at the Admiralty. He said he was calling on a matter of the gravest importance and was taking Tough into his complete confidence. 'Some help' might be needed to 'take some chaps' off the French coast, and small boats would be required—self-propelled boats, preferably fast, perhaps ten to thirty metres long, and, most importantly, not more than 1 metre draught. Could Tough find suitable candidates?

The Tough family had been building and outfitting private and pleasure boats for three generations. Their boatyard, founded in 1922, was merely the latest in the line. The Toughs were said to know every boat and boat owner on the waterway. Douglas Tough was not surprised by the request; ten days before, the BBC had broadcast a similar 'all boats' appeal to join a search for magnetic mines. And the radio news was announcing that Allied troops were falling back before German panzers on the English Channel coast.

French sailors being rescued at Dunkirk

The admiral elaborated. It might be necessary for the BEF to be evacuated by sea. This would require many boats—not only those of the British navy but private and pleasure boats of the type Tough saw and serviced every day, indeed practically any shallow-draught vessel that would float and survive a Channel crossing. The admiral asked Tough to compile a list of all the appropriate boats and their specifications, and ask the owners' permission for their use. If the owners couldn't immediately be found, Tough was authorised to commandeer the boats on behalf of the Admiralty.

Tough hardly waited to hear more. He called in his chief foreman, Harry Day. There were already fourteen boats meeting the Admiralty's needs in the boatyard. Tough put Day and his crews to work stripping the boats of peacetime amenities such as cushions and dishes, tuning the engines, filling the fuel tanks, getting the river craft ready for service at sea. Meanwhile, he gunned his own motor launch and ranged up and down the river, singling out other boats for the job and recruiting volunteer crews of weekend sailors from the local boat-owners' group, the Little Ships Club. By nightfall of 28 May, Tough's little flotilla of yachts, launches and tenders was headed downriver to join in the dramatic rescue operation that would become known as 'the Miracle of Dunkirk'.

JUST IN CASE

At the behest of the new prime minister, Winston Churchill, the Admiralty had begun mapping a just-in-case evacuation scenario on 14 May, four days after German panzers had rolled into Holland, Belgium and France. On 19 May, the Admiralty came up with a three-stage evacuation contingency plan. On 20 and 21 May, non-combat personnel—so-called 'useless mouths'— would be evacuated at a rate of two thousand a day. When they had been evacuated, fifteen thousand base personnel would follow. The third stage of the contingency plan called for three hundred thousand troops to be evacuated at the rate of forty-five thousand per day from the three Channel ports of Calais, Boulogne and Dunkirk, but initially it was given short shrift because no one expected it would be necessary.

A much-decorated officer, Vice Admiral Bertram Ramsey, was put in command. Ramsey occupied an office inside the fabled Dover chalk cliffs, tunnelled out during World War I and later used to house a dynamo that provided back-up power for Dover Castle. The plan thus became known as 'Operation Dynamo'.

No sooner had the plan been drafted than it was completely upended by events. German panzers broke through the Allied positions and drove straight for the coast in a rapid encircling movement. After pitched battles, both Calais and Boulogne were in German hands. On 28 May, the Belgian army, which had formed part of the left wing, capitulated, leaving a thirty-kilometre gap in the Allied lines and effectively pinning the BEF against the coast. Leaflets and maps dropped on the troops by the Luftwaffe summed up the Allied plight: 'British soldiers! Look at this map! It gives your true situation! Your troops are entirely surrounded—stop fighting! Put down your arms!' The British were not entirely surrounded, however. Hard-fighting Allied forces had kept open a 100-kilometre corridor to Dunkirk, now the only way out. As the broken units, scattered and straggling, headed down the corridor, across fields and through the woods, the rattled British high command faced the possible loss of its entire force.

> This would require many boats ... indeed practically any shallow-draught vessel that would float and survive a Channel crossing.

OPERATION DYNAMO COMMENCES

By now, Ramsey had 136 miscellaneous vessels at his command. They included ferries, dredges, coasters, cargo vessels, passenger steamers, even fifty self-propelled Dutch canal boats called *schuitjes* (quickly anglicised to 'scoots'), which their crews had brought across the North Sea and volunteered for Allied service. It was estimated that this fleet could evacuate forty-five thousand men in two days, after which enemy action would probably shut down the operation. As the situation darkened, at 9 pm on 26 May, the Admiralty sent a terse order: 'Operation Dynamo is to commence'. Two hours later, the first rescue vessel, *Mona's Isle*, an Isle of Man packet, set out from Dover for Dunkirk.

The Admiralty had charted three possible routes back and forth across the Channel. The shortest and best, Route X, was only thirty or so kilometres each way, but it was found to be heavily mined. So *Mona's Isle* was forced to follow Route Y, a 140-kilometre round trip. It arrived in Dunkirk at sunrise, picked up 1,400 men and returned to Dover just before 1 pm. At that rate and at that load level, it would take sixty days to evacuate the whole force. Clearly more boats were needed.

The navy then sent nine of its destroyers and a squadron of minesweepers, which could pull up to the Dunkirk pier and load. But the Luftwaffe's Stuka dive-bombers made short work of them. Many were sunk or were so heavily damaged they could not be used, and their half-submerged hulks blocked other ships from reaching the pier. The pier itself became a wreck. While some ships continued to scoop men off the mole, attention shifted to a sixteen-kilometre stretch of sand east of Dunkirk. Thousands of soldiers gathered there, awaiting the ships that were sure to save them. Forming orderly queues reaching into the surf, they stayed calm, and their belief in the Royal Navy never flagged: after all, the navy had evacuated the troops at Gallipoli in 1915, hadn't it?

Moving to the beaches presented another problem, however. The Flemish coast has 'shelved' beaches, distinguished by gradual changes in water depth. Large vessels such as destroyers, minesweepers and transports could only approach within

> Gathered, too ... were clusters of volunteer crewmen who had answered a call for amateur sailors. Many had rushed straight from home or work to sign up.

2 kilometres of shore. Small boats that skimmed the surface were needed to shuttle troops to the big ships—hence the appeal to Tough for boats with a shallow draught.

British and French troops waiting to be picked up from the beach east of Dunkirk, in June 1940

HERE COME THE WEEKEND SAILORS

The small armada that had set out from Tough's boatyard went first to Sheerness, a small port on the Thames Estuary that had been designated the meeting point. There they were joined by a hodgepodge of other boats: glistening yachts with their brightwork polished, lifeboats that had been stripped from coastal steamers, fishing smacks, cabin cruisers, speedboats, launches. The entire cockle-shell fleet from Leigh-on-Sea had turned out. One of the Thames's shallow-draught fireboats and its crew had volunteered. Gathered, too, at Sheerness were clusters of volunteer crewmen who had answered a call for amateur sailors. Many had rushed straight from home or work to sign up. Men from the financial services of the City still in their cutaways and striped trousers mingled with grizzled seamen and navy sublieutenants just out of training school. Many had never been to sea before; some had never set foot in a boat.

From Sheerness, the fleet moved on to Ramsgate at the mouth of the Thames, where their fuel tanks were topped up, supplies were loaded and they were grouped into convoys. They were issued compasses and nautical charts on which the routes to Dunkirk were marked. There were not enough charts for everyone, so some skippers were given travel brochures bearing drawings of the French coast. At 10 pm on 29 May, the first convoy pushed off. 'Close up and follow me', commanded Royal Navy Lieutenant R.H. Irving, and away they went. Though the Channel had a reputation for heavy swells, rough seas and treacherous currents, that night it was 'smooth as glass', as one skipper reported later. There was, however, a heavy mist, but this redounded to the ships' benefit, since it kept much of the Luftwaffe on the ground.

Lieutenant Ian Cox of the destroyer *Malcolm* was bringing his third load of troops back to Dover that day when the dawn disclosed a strange sight. Ahead of him he saw a mass of black specks on the surface of the sea. As the specks came closer, he recognised them as vessels—dozens of vessels of every imaginable kind. The Teddington armada was among them, Tough himself steering his motor launch. Realising their mission and their bravery, Cox felt so proud that he burst out with the Saint Crispin's Day speech from Shakespeare's *Henry V*: 'And Gentlemen in England now abed / Shall think themselves accurs'd they were not here'.

Nearing the coast, the men in the boats saw some strange sights, too. The long stretch of white sand seemed dotted with shrubbery. The shrubs moved and turned out to be men. Long lines of them stretched into the sea. Makeshift jetties constructed from beached and abandoned trucks parked end to end in the surf were crowded with men. Some had been standing for hours, holding their place in the line.

The little ships were to approach as closely as possible to the beach, gather up whatever troops they could carry and ferry them to the minesweepers, destroyers and transports waiting offshore. Tough and his men found it no easy task. Troops able to breast the heavy surf swam out and tried to climb into the boats. Trying to lift an exhausted man in watersoaked clothes and boots filled with sand was backbreaking work. Sometimes so many anxious men tried to climb aboard at once that the boat capsized. After a few such episodes, the rescue crews learned the secret of ferrying: get close enough to shore to pick up men but not so close as to be swamped by hordes afraid of being left behind; on a large vessel, help the bone-tired men to ascend the landing nets.

Making repeated trips under the threat of bombing and machine-gun fire, working hour after hour, the small ships gradually cleared the beaches. By the end of 30 May, a total of 29,512 men had been saved, more than a third of them rescued by the little ships.

EVERY MAN FOR HIMSELF

But there were still men waiting, and more coming. The French and British forces had kept the escape corridor open as long as possible, but now were forced to fall back to protect the evacuation itself. The final units reached safety, but still came a flood of stragglers, men who had been told, 'It's every man for himself! Make for Dunkirk!' They had been bedded down in the woods, holed up in farmhouses, taking shelter in shattered buildings. Individuals separated from their units now staggered forwards to join the evacuation, numbering in the thousands. It was decided to close down the operation at sunrise on 1 June. As the decision was made, 45,000 men were still waiting to embark.

So the little ships came back again, albeit in smaller numbers— many skippers had decided they had done their bit and had headed home; others had been damaged in collisions. The remaining

There was, however, a heavy mist, but this redounded to the ships' benefit, since it kept much of the Luftwaffe on the ground.

boats were, however, augmented by what Admiral Ramsey called 'freelances'. Until 30 May, the government had keep a tight lid on news of the evacuation. Once the news was out, little ships from ports all along the coast joined in the rescue effort, often without bothering to notify Operation Dynamo.

At dawn on 1 June, the curtain officially came down. General Harold Alexander, commanding the truncated BEF, cruised the coast, shouting through a megaphone, 'Is anybody there?' Satisfied no one was being left, he called quits to Operation Dynamo.

Alexander reckoned without the redoubtable Winston Churchill, however. The prime minister had pledged that British and French would be evacuated in roughly equal numbers. Yet of the 165,000 lifted off by sunrise on 1 June, only 15,000 were French. Churchill insisted that the worn-out men and ships should return for two more days. On 2 and 3 June, another 46,431 soldiers were taken off the coast, more than three-quarters of them French. The total of evacuees was 364,628, including 224,686 members of the BEF.

The skippers and crews of the Teddington 'little ships' returned home, sailing up the Thames with other members of the miniature armada, along riverbanks lined with crowds cheering them as heroes. In the next days, the newspapers, the House of Commons and Prime Minister Churchill's speeches all paid tribute to the 'Miracle of Dunkirk'. In Teddington, meanwhile, Douglas Tough was back in his boatyard, looking out at the peaceful Thames.

The Pedlar, the Fox and the Rats

The Siege of Tobruk

The ageing, battered Italian fishing schooner *Maria Giovanni* edged along the darkened Libyan coastline, guiding itself by the headlights of trucks rumbling along the Italian desert colony's only highway. On deck, the burly commander of the vessel glanced sometimes at the shore, sometimes at his compass, meanwhile scanning the skies and listening for enemy aircraft. He hardly resembled a sea-gnarled Italian fisherman, and he wasn't: the officer's cap pulled low over his eyes carried the insignia of the Royal Navy.

The *Maria Giovanni*'s skipper peered intently ahead, his eyes seeking a dim but familiar green light flashing from a headland on the ship's port side. Its glow would designate the entrance to the harbour of Tobruk, on Libya's Mediterranean shore. Ah, there it was! The skipper deftly steered the craft through the narrow harbour entrance, manoeuvring around the shadowy hulks of broken or damaged, half-sunk and bombed-out vessels. The *Maria Giovanni* glided up to a shattered jetty, where a cluster of the skipper's Australian countrymen eagerly waited. After the boat was moored, they systematically unloaded its cargo—barrels and drums of food, ammunition, fuel, mail and 'the odd bottle of rum'. That welcome supply would help them to endure what would soon become the longest siege of the Western war. Choked off from land resupply by an encircling force of Germans and Italians,

... barrels and drums of food, ammunition, fuel, mail and 'the odd bottle of rum'. That welcome supply would help them to endure what would soon become the longest siege of the Western war.

Allied artillery firing on German
positions during the fighting to
control Tobruk

they knew that their very lives depended on the gutsiness of men like the captain of the *Maria Giovanni*.

That intrepid skipper's name was Alfred Brian Palmer, but few people ever called him that. Born in 1898 on a farm west of Sydney, early in life he had been nicknamed for a popular boxer, Pedlar Palmer, who had fought a much wagered-upon world title fight with the champion, Terry McGovern, in 1899. Palmer was knocked out in the first minute of the first round, probably bankrupting not a few backers. But the nickname stuck, and when Palmer the seafarer turned up like clockwork with shiploads of everything from livestock to shaving cream, 'Pedlar' seemed an appropriate sobriquet. Since the *Maria Giovanni* was a sailing vessel armed with two small-bore cannon that Palmer sometimes fired at other ships or shore installations, some of the Tobruk garrison also took to calling him 'the Pirate'. Palmer the buccaneer responded by occasionally flying the black skull-and-crossbones from his mainmast. It was only one of the ways he often dismayed his superiors.

'You are caught like rats in a trap', the renegade American-born broadcaster Lord Haw-Haw chortled from Berlin.

BACK AND FORTH ACROSS THE DESERT

Following the Italian attack on Egypt, the British, though outnumbered five to one, mounted a robust response. They were determined to maintain control of North Africa, for it provided access to the Suez Canal (and thence Asia), the imperial Middle East domain and the oilfields of the Persian Gulf. After twice halting the Italian forces near the Egyptian border, in early February 1941, the army of General Richard O'Connor swept 650 kilometres across the forbidding desert of Libya behind the befuddled Italian armies, pinning them against the sea at the port of Benghazi and taking 130,000 prisoners. That represented practically the entire Italian colonial force—a disastrous black eye for Italy.

Within a few days, however, Italy's Axis ally Germany sent in General Erwin Rommel, who would earn the nickname of 'the Desert Fox', followed by his *Afrika Korps* and panzer divisions. A far cry from the demoralised Italians, they smashed eastwards from Benghazi. By March 1941, the Allies, weakened by the withdrawal of fifty-eight thousand men dispatched to support their allies in Greece, were in headlong retreat. Some of the Allies retired towards another port, Tobruk, which the Australian Ninth Division had seized earlier. The sardonic Australians called their hasty retreat 'the Benghazi–Tobruk Handicap'.

Most Allied troops then fell back towards Egypt. But Tobruk, a key port and protection for the island bastion of Malta, was too important to give up, and the soldiers there, mainly the Australian Ninth Division, a brigade from the Australian Seventh Division and elements of two tank divisions, were told to stay put. On 6 April 1941, Rommel and his men surrounded the town. 'You are caught like rats in a trap', the renegade American-born broadcaster Lord Haw-Haw chortled from Berlin. Unperturbed, the 'Rats of Tobruk' gloried in this name and soon made it their own.

'NO SURRENDER AND NO RETREAT'

Tobruk was a cluster of whitewashed mud structures on a promontory above the Mediterranean Sea. It was surrounded by head-high trenches and antitank traps and dug-in pillboxes. 'You must hold out for eight weeks', the Middle East Allied commander, Field Marshal Archibald Wavell, told the Australian commander, Lieutenant General Leslie Morshead. Wavell envisioned his colonials and troops returning from Greece and regrouping for another onslaught across North Africa. Tobruk would be the jumping-off place. Meanwhile, the garrison would be reinforced and supplied by sea. 'There will be no Dunkirk here', warned Morshead. 'There is to be no surrender and no retreat.'

Rommel saw Tobruk as crucial to his plans, too. He could not afford to bypass a port where the mighty British navy could land a threatening force in his rear. Over Easter, he launched two titanic attacks against the Rats of Tobruk, but was stymied by the doughty Australians. After devastating losses on both sides in pitched, hand-to-hand battles, Rommel settled in for a siege. He was convinced that night-and-day bombing and strafing by the Luftwaffe, plus air and ship attacks on resupply vessels, would soon bring the hungry garrison to its knees.

The Allies saw the same picture. Wavell and Morshead were to keep Rommel occupied so his *Afrika Korps* could not join the fighting elsewhere. Accordingly, Morshead rejected a purely defensive strategy in favour of sending nightly armed patrols into the Axis lines, both to probe for weak spots and to hint that the Allies might be attempting a breakout. Meanwhile, they would depend on what the Australians called 'the spud run', and the likes of Pedlar Palmer, to keep the garrison fed and armed.

A HUNDRED DAYS AROUND THE HORN

Palmer had had a chequered life since leaving home at the height of World War I. Aged eighteen, he signed on to a sailing vessel that took him to France. There he joined the Royal Navy, serving on minelayers and destroyers. After the Armistice, he went back to merchant shipping, and wound up in Shanghai. He achieved a position as chief steward of the posh Shanghai Club, reputed to have the longest bar in the world. Rubbing elbows with the elite of the international community, he soon became a partner in a shipping firm and director of a bank.

As hostilities heightened between Japan and China, Palmer the ex-military man was chosen to lead a mounted troop of Chinese Lancers, which was affiliated with the American Volunteer Troop

and armed to protect Shanghai's International Settlement. But when Britain declared war on Germany in September 1939, Palmer, as a naval reservist, was immediately called to the British consulate. 'There is a state of war and we are mobilising ex-servicemen from around the world', he was told. 'His Majesty the King would appreciate your services.' Within two weeks, Palmer was in Hong Kong wearing a naval lieutenant's stripes. 'I was probably the only man to hold a commission in the American Volunteer Troop and the Royal Navy at one and the same time', he recalled later.

Some of the Australian 'Rats of Tobruk' taking refuge in tunnels at the height of the siege

He went on to Singapore, Ceylon (now Sri Lanka) and finally through the Suez Canal to Alexandria as executive officer of a submarine tender, the *Medway*. In Alexandria, he was given command of three A-lighters, flat-bottomed vessels that were the forerunners of tank landing craft. Palmer's 'flagship', the *A-39*, joined the naval Inshore Squadron, first running supplies to the armies advancing across the desert, then to Tobruk when the siege began. One day in port, he noticed three Italian sailing vessels that the Royal Navy had commandeered. Why couldn't they be turned into blockade runners to supply the embattled Tobruk garrison, he asked. As a result, Palmer, one of the few Royal Navy officers with experience in seagoing sailing vessels, was named skipper of the *Maria Giovanni* in January 1941.

He commanded a 55-metre-long, 300-tonne, three-masted vessel with a crew of twelve. It could make six knots, twice the speed of the old *A-39*, and could carry 180 tonnes of miscellaneous cargo. And a miscellaneous cargo it was. The decks were frequently crowded with bleating sheep, transported for the Indian troops who could not stomach the standard fare of bully beef. Once, Palmer brought out to Alexandria a shipload of camp-following Italian prostitutes, left behind in their army's hasty flight. On

MEANWHILE, DOWN SOUTH ...

Benito Mussolini had long dreamed of being a new Caesar, and ruling over a new Roman empire. But by 1941, that dream was rapidly fading. In January, the British launched a three-pronged attack on Italian East Africa and within two months had completely routed the Italian defenders and restored deposed king Haile Selassie to his throne in Addis Ababa. In some cases, the attackers could scarcely keep up with the retreating defenders. One of the last to give up was the Italian commander in Somaliland, who burst into tears when required to turn over his pistol to the British commander. The Briton patted him on the shoulder, with the comforting words: 'War can be very embarrassing'. Mussolini could have said the same.

another occasion, he transported sixty-four Australian and British nurses from Tobruk to a hospital ship—'The best-looking cargo we ever carried', he said. The troops loved him because he brought mail and never failed to supply beer.

NAVIGATING 'BOMB ALLEY'

The shipping lane between Alexandria and Tobruk was nicknamed 'Bomb Alley'. Both the lane and Tobruk itself were under constant aerial and artillery attack. The once-picturesque harbour became littered with twisted wreckage and half-sunk ships, and the town a shattered collection of ruined buildings. Palmer quickly developed zigzag and figure-eight manoeuvres to avoid the bombs and machine-gun fire. Working close to the shore, he would lurk beneath sandstorms, hoping that his masts would not poke above the screen of dust. To further foil the attackers, the *Maria Giovanni* travelled mostly at night. The Germans were fully aware of its comings and goings, and the Italians put a price on 'the Pirate's' head. 'We will get you yet, Palmer', Lord Haw-Haw boasted from Berlin.

The fortress itself became a honeycomb of underground tunnels and chambers, where the troops trudged around barefoot and in cut-off uniform shorts—fifty-degree Tobruk was no place for spit and polish. They conducted running chess games, drank beer when they could get it, wrote letters home, fought off voracious flies and frequently defied the menacing aircraft to bask on the beaches and splash in their waters. They even published their own newspaper, *The Dinkum Oil* (from the Australian terms *dinkum*, 'genuine', and *good oil*, 'reliable information'). The nightly probes and the shelling gradually took a toll, however.

Against Wavell's and Morshead's advice, Churchill insisted on an attempt to break the siege, and in May 1941 dispatched the 'Tiger Convoy' to ferry 295 tanks and 53 aircraft to Egypt. Nearing

> The shipping lane between Alexandria and Tobruk was nicknamed 'Bomb Alley'. Both the lane and Tobruk itself were under constant aerial and artillery attack.

shore, however, two of the ships hit mines and blew up, taking with them to the bottom fifty-seven tanks and ten planes. In a subsequent offensive launched on 14 June 1941, and named Battleaxe, tanks were to smash across the border into Libya and the Tobruk garrison break out to link up with them. The Australians waited for the order, but were then told their advance had been postponed. In fact, Rommel had uncovered the British plan and was ready for the tanks. The battle went on for three days before the British withdrew back across the border.

After the failure of Battleaxe, Wavell was replaced by General Claude Auchinleck. The new commander also cautiously continued to delay, suggesting that, with more troops and more tanks, Tobruk might be relieved by the end of the year. Meanwhile, the garrison was to stay put. That was too much for the Australian government. It protested to Churchill that the Australians were being sacrificed for no discernible goal and should be relieved forthwith. Initially, Churchill ignored the entreaties, but then he decided to replace the battered Australians. They had served him well, keeping the *Afrika Korps* pinned down for six months, preventing their bolstering the Russian front, and stymieing Rommel's hope for a drive to the Suez Canal.

Through September and October, three replacement brigades of Polish troops were brought in through the blockade, and unit by unit, the Australians were evacuated. By mid-October, all fourteen thousand 'rats' had said goodbye to Tobruk. The siege went on, however, and it wasn't until 12 December 1941, that Auchinleck's Eighth Army, with new divisions and rejuvenated armoured columns, drove Rommel's forces backwards again and freed the embattled city after a blockade of 282 days. Rommel, however, was to seize the initiative again, recapture Tobruk and surge into Egypt before a reinforced Eighth Army under General Bernard L. Montgomery would halt him at El Alamein.

Nearing shore, however, two of the ships hit mines and blew up, taking with them to the bottom fifty-seven tanks and ten planes.

RUN AGROUND

After his fellow Australians were evacuated, Palmer continued to supply the Tobruk garrison. Then, in November 1941, he was outfoxed himself. Sneaking as usual along the coast to enter Tobruk harbour under cover of darkness, he spotted what he thought was his green welcome light and swung to port. Unfortunately, the enemy had installed a decoy light, and he was 'welcomed' by the crunch of sand as the *Maria Giovanni* ran aground. The Italians arrived at daylight and Palmer was captured and sent to a prisoner of war camp in Italy, where he spent nearly two years.

After Italy's surrender, prisoners were transferred by train to camps in Germany. En route, Palmer, ever daring, saw his chance. He entered the lavatory, pried open a window and squeezed out, landing on the tracks. His escape set off an alarm and he was quickly surrounded by guards and peppered with a fusillade of bullets. One caught him in the elbow and shattered the joint. When he awoke in a prison hospital, his left arm had been amputated below the shoulder. Not wanting to be burdened by a useless hospital case, authorities arranged for his repatriation to England. By then, late 1944, most of the well-fed 'Rats of Tobruk' were fighting against the Japanese. After a triumphal tour of the United States and a post-war revisit to his old haunts in Shanghai and Hong Kong, Palmer returned to Australia as a hero, if an unusual one.

The Road of Life

Surviving the Siege of Leningrad

Winter night begins early in the northern latitudes, and at 3 pm on 19 November 1941, darkness had already closed in. Mikhail Murov, captain of a Soviet transport regiment, and his crew were working under sullen skies to repair the outer defences of Leningrad, the Soviet Union's second largest city. A messenger came up to Murov with an order. He and his unit were to report immediately to the Leningrad freight station.

Murov was puzzled. As far as he knew, no trains were running out of Leningrad. The Germans had steadily and inexorably tightened their noose around the city, cutting the last rail connection to Moscow on 30 August and capturing the last road into the city a week later. In September, they had abandoned their nonstop artillery bombardment in favour of a new strategy: starvation of the city's two-and-a-half million people. ('Why waste bombs and shells?' Colonel-General Franz Halder, chief of the general staff, had asked.) German warships had established an impenetrable blockade around the port. Leningrad was by now almost totally isolated, cut off from all the necessities of life. Coal for the power stations and the railroads was dwindling fast and could not be replenished. Daily bread rations had been reduced four times since 8 September. Murov had been informed a few hours earlier that they would be cut again on 23 November, to 150 grams a day—just a few slices, barely enough to sustain life.

Murov's men were primarily 'People's Volunteers', part of the hordes who had come forward or been conscripted to prepare Leningrad for a possible ground onslaught. The volunteers had

Leningraders growing vegetables in a square

already dug kilometres of trenches and tank traps, built pillboxes and concrete machine-gun nests, cleared brush for fields of fire and ringed most of the fortifications with barbed wire—Murov's group's particular responsibility. After receiving his latest order, Murov allowed a few of his men who lived nearby to rush home and say farewells. Then, their footfalls muffled by the snow, they marched through the empty streets to the railway station.

THE FROZEN LAKE

The temperature was at minus eighteen Celsius as Murov's men and other units piled into unheated coaches. Huddled together for warmth, they endured a bumpy, chilling, overnight journey to awaken at the tiny fishing village of Kokkorevo on the shores of Lake Ladoga. The largest but arguably least-known lake in Europe, Ladoga formed the northern and northeastern boundary of the Leningrad Oblast, or province. Measuring 200 miles long and 1,300 kilometres across, it is 200 metres deep in some places, but markedly shallow near the Leningrad side. The shoreline was then the site of a few small settlements like Kokkorevo, and here and there an old monastery or pre-Revolutionary estate, but was mostly cranberry bogs and timber. In summer, ferries and fishing boats plied the lake. But what Murov and his men saw in November was a shimmering sheet of glass: Ladoga was frozen over from shore to shore.

Soviet officials had been anxiously and nervously watching the lake's surface for days. Records showed that ice usually began to form by 19 November, and would gradually reach a thickness of one to two metres. Twenty-four consecutive days of minus five degrees Celsius or less would produce thirty centimetres of ice; eight days at minus fifteen degrees did the same. Ten centimetres of ice would support a horse without a load, eighteen centimetres a horse-drawn sledge with a one-tonne load, twenty centimetres a

Leningrad was by now almost totally isolated, cut off from all the necessities of life. Coal for the power stations and the railroads was dwindling fast and could not be replenished.

truck carrying a tonne. The officials had driven a scout car across the lake the day before and the ice had borne its weight.

They told transport officer Murov his assignment. He was to lead a column of horsedrawn sledges across the ice to the opposite shore. There the sledges would be loaded with food, kerosene and petrol and taken back across the ice for the hungry population of Leningrad—virtually the first supplies to reach the beleaguered city in more than two months. 'The ice is very young, and not very strong', a Soviet commissar said despairingly to Murov. But Leningrad had supplies for only two more days. After that the cupboard was bare; the people of Leningrad would starve. 'We can't wait', the commissar said. An emergency 'ice road' over Ladoga was the only hope. Otherwise, the great city would die.

It was a daunting task. Murov had 350 men, but most were truck drivers, not teamsters. The horses themselves were ragged and weak, barely able to pull even an unloaded sledge. Like the humans, they had been on a starvation diet since the siege began. Many of them, Murov thought, were too feeble to survive an arduous pull across the ice in zero weather. He had visions of the horses dropping dead on the ice, upending the sledges with them. But as the commissar had said, there was no other choice. Anything less than a heroic effort would mean a death sentence for two-and-a-half million people.

BLAZING A TRAIL

The scouting party had marked a 50-kilometre route across the ice, planting flags in the ice to mark soft spots and detours. Murov's column set out along it at early light. The column stretched out for nearly eight kilometres, with the sledges roughly thirty metres apart, so as not to concentrate weight on the still-fragile ice. The sky was overcast and the temperatures around minus eighteen;

chilling winds blew across the lake. In their hasty departure, many drivers had not been issued winter jackets and now huddled against the cold. At an island in the middle of the lake, the caravan stopped for a two-hour rest. The men each received a ration of bread and a mug of tea laced with sugar. There was no forage for the horses, so some of the men shared their bread with the animals.

At mid-evening, the column reached Kobona on the opposite shore, where a warehouse had hastily been built to store supplies. The men received another welcome meal, of hardtack, macaroni and cottonseed-oil cakes. But the expected supply of oats and bran for the horses did not materialise. Murov was desperate. He could not believe the weakened animals would survive another fifty-kilometre trip in polar temperatures while pulling heavy loads. He scraped back some of the snow to find old grass underneath. He put his men to work uncovering the grass for the animals. At least that would be something.

Then the sledges were loaded with flour and food concentrates and the return journey began. In the early-morning hours of 22 November, the long troupe reached Kokkorevo and the Leningrad side. It brought only a few tonnes of food—all that the frail horses would be counted upon to pull—but the 'ice road' that spelled relief was open, and carrying lifesaving traffic. Officially, it was now designated Military Motorway 101. But Leningraders dubbed it *Doroga Zhizni*, the 'Road of Life'.

STARVING IN THE DARK

The Road of Life, however, was scarcely enough to keep the city fed and warm. After three months of what they called the *blokaden*, Leningraders huddled in cold and darkened apartments without electricity, heating oil or communications. There was no power, so radio stations could not broadcast. Newspapers

stopped publishing; no one was available—or strong enough—to lift or distribute bundles of newspapers. Even those who had a few morsels of food could not cook it. Most couldn't work, either; even if they felt healthy enough, most factories were closed. Without fuel, machines couldn't operate. Trams and buses stopped running; some were simply abandoned in the streets. Leningrad's boulevards were not only empty of cars, but of people. The art treasures of the fabled Hermitage Museum were stored in underground vaults to protect them from shelling. The vaults doubled as air-raid shelters.

That first winter, Leningrad's was a life of unspeakable privation. Half the population—those who survived—suffered from dystrophy, wasting of muscle tissue brought on by poor nutrition.

A woman dragging a child's body along a busy Leningrad street, at the height of the siege

With no food to be had in the shops, people turned to whatever they could locate, cook and eat. The pigeons disappeared from the city parks, having been captured and served for dinner, along with the ubiquitous crows. People guiltily resorted to eating pet dogs, cats and even canaries. There were rumours, never confirmed, of cannibalism. Children's sleds, once the enjoyable staple of a Leningrad winter, were put to a new and macabre use: the transport of frozen corpses to city cemeteries. So many were dying of hunger and cold that they could not be buried in the frozen turf, even if there were gravediggers. Bodies were stacked up—'like cordwood', a mortician said—at cemetery gates, awaiting the end of the *blokaden*, the spring thaw or healthy gravediggers—whichever came first. Trees in the city's parks had been chopped down to fuel fireplaces and cooking stoves. A new and frightening form of crime sprang up: murder for food, or for ration cards.

Yet Leningrad struggled on. People even made jokes about their plight. One man introduced his wife as his 'better quarter'. 'She used to be my better half', he said, 'but she's lost so much weight, she's now only twenty-five per cent.' A writers' group resolutely continued its weekly meetings in the catacombs under

RUNNING THE GAUNTLET

As trucks and sledges brought food to Leningrad, the Allies set up another relief mission to the Soviet Union, with its own risks. U.S. shipments of armaments, tanks, trucks, jeeps, aircraft, clothing, rations and locomotives were sent across the North Atlantic to the ice-free port of Murmansk on the Arctic Ocean, often with tragic results. German U-boat attacks made the route the most dangerous of all shipping lanes—in the first six months of 1942, two-thirds of ships bound for Murmansk were picked off by German submarines. The situation would improve in 1943, thanks to improved intelligence and the employment of armed escort ships, allowing a huge flow of supplies to reach the Soviets for the remainder of the war.

the Hermitage. Its ink supply froze, but the writers used their breath to warm it up. The composer Dimitri Shostakovich, a Leningrad native, refused to leave the city and became a fire warden, combatting the incendiaries that Germans rained on the city. He wrote the first three movements of his Seventh Symphony during the *blokaden*. When the work was finished, he dedicated it to the courageous people of Leningrad. But when the time came for its initial performance in March 1942, there were too few surviving or healthy members of the Leningrad Radio Orchestra, so it was first performed in the temporary capital of Kuybyshev (now Samara), and then in Moscow on 29 March 1942. Leningrad did not hear it until six months later, on 7 August.

In the first weeks of the Road of Life, Murov and his crews were able to transport 770 tonnes of supplies, scarcely two days' worth even at the 125-gram level. The minimum needed was 900 tonnes, it was estimated, including kerosene and petrol. For three weeks, horses and men stumbled back and forth across the ice but most days could fulfil only about half the needs. But as the ice thickened and became stronger, Murov found himself back at the wheel of a truck. Sledges gave way to tonne-and-a-half trucks, then to three-tonne vehicles, some capable of sixty kilometres an hour, that could make two round trips a day.

The Military Motorway grew into a superhighway, with sixty routes and lanes, and a total length of sixteen hundred kilometres. The Road of Life sprouted first-aid stations, repair facilities, rest stops, snow-clearing crews and even traffic police. Soon it became a two-way street: rather than return to Kobona empty, the sledges and trucks began to bring out the sick, the elderly, pregnant women and children to shelter on the far shore. Ultimately, 514,000 civilians and 35,000 wounded soldiers were evacuated in this way.

People guiltily resorted to eating pet dogs, cats and even canaries. There were rumours, never confirmed, of cannibalism.

German artillery and aircraft soon found the range of the road and bombed it incessantly. The cross-ice trip was often one of zigzags and quick twists and turns to avoid bomb craters or strafing. The drivers strove valiantly to make the daily quota. Murov warned them, 'If you are late with your trip, a thousand people could die'.

FRUIT FOR THE CHILDREN

The driver Maxim Tverdokhleb was loading his truck one late December night in 1941 when he noticed that some plywood crates seemed extraordinarily light. They also exuded a tempting aroma. The crates were labelled 'For the Heroic Children of Leningrad!' Children in the republic of Georgia were shipping tangerines to Leningrad as New Year gifts. It happened to be a bright, moonlit night, illuminating the road for German aircraft. Tverdokhleb had hardly begun when two planes bore down on his truck, spouting bullets. They shot out the windshield, riddled the truckbed, hit the radiator and wounded the driver's arm. Tverdokhleb was determined. 'I could have jumped out and escaped but what would have become of the children's tangerines? So I thought, "No, I will make it there!"' When he arrived at the Leningrad side, forty-nine bullet holes were counted in the truck. But the tangerines were safe.

The Road of Life officially closed down on 24 April 1942, as the ice gradually melted; boats took over the supply route and continued during the summer. By then, more than two hundred thousand Leningraders had died of starvation or illness. How many others were saved from an agonising death by the meagre foodstuffs brought across the ice, or by being taken to safety and care beyond the siege, could never be counted.

The Road of Life was opened again the following December, and Murov and his crews steered their vehicles across Lake Ladoga

> German artillery and aircraft soon found the range of the road and bombed it incessantly.

again. In January 1943, a two-pronged Soviet offensive punched a hole through the besieging German lines, partially lifting the siege and sending Leningraders into the streets in mad celebration. It was a little premature, however: the attack opened only a narrow corridor, and trucks and trains could only operate under heavy bombardment from both sides. The ice road was still needed. On 24 April 1943, the government completed an oil supply pipeline under the lake to bring fuel oil to the besieged and chilled city, which also relieved some pressure on the Road of Life.

The siege of Leningrad would go on for nine hundred days, until 27 January 1944, when a major Soviet drive under Marshal Georgy Zhukov forced the Germans to pull out and into full retreat. Throughout that terrible time, Mikhail Murov, along with most of the other citizens of Leningrad, had held fast to the belief that 'The Neva [Leningrad's river] will flow upstream before this city surrenders'. And ultimately he, and they, could assert with satisfaction: 'Troy fell. Rome fell. Leningrad did not fall'.

Payback Time

America Gets Even for Pearl Harbor

ike most of the proud American navy—like most Americans—Captain Francis Lowe felt angered and humiliated by the devastating Japanese attack on Pearl Harbor, which had destroyed or heavily damaged eight main-line battleships and other naval vessels, wiped out 188 planes and damaged 155 others, and left 2,300 servicemen killed and 1,100 wounded, along with more than 100 civilians. The raid had delivered a shattering blow to America's complacent 'It can't happen here' mentality and sent a shiver through the whole country. 'A date that will live in infamy', as President Roosevelt had ringingly termed it, called for America to strike back. But how? It was a question that Lowe and many others pondered in the dark days of December 1941.

The Japanese attack, launched from aircraft carriers, had taught a clear and painful lesson: the future of naval warfare, especially in the vast reaches of the Pacific, lay not with duelling battleships, but with carriers being used to launch devastating air attacks on enemy fleets at sea or at their bases. Fortunately, although America's 'Battleship Row' was in ruins after Pearl Harbor, American aircraft carriers had been spared—most had been at sea or at ports on the Pacific Coast on the day of the attack. To bolster this force, the U.S. Navy had already been frantically building two new high-speed carriers at its naval shipyard in Norfolk, Virginia, and just as frantically training crews to man them. Captain Lowe was on the staff of Admiral Ernest J. King, the navy's commander in chief in Washington. In early January, he was dispatched to Norfolk to review the construction and outfitting of the new carriers.

Lowe found Norfolk abuzz with war preparations. On one runway had been painted the two-hundred-metre outline of an aircraft-carrier deck. Lowe watched dive-bombers, torpedo bombers, pursuit ships and fighter aircraft as their pilots practised landings and takeoffs in that limited space. Lowe was a submariner who had never flown. Nonetheless, as he watched, a daring idea took shape in his mind: Why couldn't fast carriers approach the Japanese mainland and launch a bomber attack on Tokyo? Why couldn't America defiantly strike back right at the heart of the Japanese nation, and wipe those smug smiles off Japanese faces?

JUST THE MAN FOR THE JOB

As soon as Lowe returned to Washington on 14 January, he went directly to King's office and presented his idea. King was another ex-submariner, but he had learned to fly and had risen through the aviation side of the navy; before being named to the navy's top job, he had commanded the aircraft carrier *Lexington*. King, like America's other top brass, was being pressed by Roosevelt to do something bold, and Lowe's brainstorm was certainly appealing. King summoned his air-operations officer, Captain Donald Duncan, and told him to investigate Lowe's idea.

Two days later, Duncan returned with his findings. To have any chance of success, he said, the carriers would have to take the planes within 500 kilometres of Tokyo. Carrier-based, single-engine navy bombers didn't have the range nor the bomb- and fuel-carrying capacity for the mission. But, Duncan suggested, twin-engine bombers did. That they had never taken off from a short carrier deck was trifling. Pilots could learn, couldn't they?

Admiral King at once picked up the phone and called his U.S. Air Force counterpart, General Henry 'Hap' Arnold. Arnold—also under pressure—was intrigued by the idea and said he knew just the man to carry it out: Lieutenant Colonel James H. Doolittle.

... the devastating Japanese attack on Pearl Harbor, which had destroyed or heavily damaged eight main-line battleships and other naval vessels, wiped out 188 planes and damaged 155 others ...

Crew members watching a B-25
take off from the deck of the
Hornet, en route to bomb Tokyo

Jimmy Doolittle had been a famous Air Corps stunt, racing and test pilot during the barnstorming days of 1920s and 1930s aviation. In 1922, he had become the first pilot to fly across the States in less than twenty-four hours. He held a world speed record (for the time) of 395 kilometres per hour; he was the first pilot to fly an outside loop (one in which the cockpit is on the outside of the circle), in a Curtiss Hawk biplane, in 1927; he held a shelf full of trophies from air shows and races across the country. Doolittle had also pioneered 'blind' flying, which involved navigating a set course using only instruments while sealed into a completely enclosed cockpit. On top of all that, he held master's and doctoral degrees in aeronautical science. Arnold directed Doolittle to investigate Lowe's idea from both a pilot's and an aeronautical engineer's point of view. And to do it post-haste, and secretly.

Doolittle came back in a few days with a detailed report. The plan was absolutely feasible, using the air force's twin-engine B-25 Mitchell medium bomber. It could carry up to a tonne of bombs fully loaded and still lift off at low speed well within the length of a carrier deck. By adding a 1000-litre leakproof fuel tank over the bomb bay, a second, inflatable tank above that and another tank in place of the bottom machine-gun turret, the plane's range could be extended to 2000 kilometres. Unfortunately, the B-25 was too big to land on a carrier, but the extended range would allow it to reach Japan and continue to friendly airfields in China. The B-25 crews could certainly be trained for carrier takeoffs. Indeed, they could be ready by 1 April. Doolittle volunteered to lead the flight himself.

UP, UP AND AWAY

Armed with a top-priority from Arnold and backed by Roosevelt and Chief of Staff George C. Marshall, Doolittle set out to make the plan work. On 3 February, he had two B-25 pilots,

Lieutenants John Fitzgerald and James McCarthy, make more than thirty short-distance takeoffs to prove how readily it could be done, then did the same on a carrier 160 kilometres offshore. He assembled 25 volunteer crews and gathered them together at a secret base at Eglin Field, Florida. He warned the flyers not to mention the mission or training to anyone. 'This will be an extremely hazardous mission requiring a high degree of skill', Doolittle told them. 'It could be of great value to the war effort. Anyone who wants to drop out, can, and no questions asked.' He repeated the offer many times over the next weeks, but no one ever left.

Doolittle himself had never flown a twin-engine plane off a carrier deck, and insisted on undergoing the same training as the other flyers. Meanwhile, engineers and mechanics set to work refitting the B-25s. Extraneous features were removed to make way for the extra fuel tanks and bomb racks. Since secrecy and radio silence would be critical, even cumbersome communications equipment was scrapped. A 1942-vintage B-25 lacked a gun turret in the tail; the ordnance officer, Captain Ross Greening, obtained two long broomsticks for each plane, painted them black and installed them in the tail to confuse any pursuing Japanese. The B-25s carried a secretly developed Norden bombsight, which locked the plane on an undeviating path to the target once it was in the crosshairs. But it was designed for use at high altitude, and Doolittle planned to bring the bombers over Japanese cities at only six hundred metres. Besides, if a plane were shot down, the secret sight might fall into the hands of the Japanese. Out went the Norden bombsight. To replace it, Greening designed a makeshift version he named a 'Mark Twain', for the depth-sounding apparatus used by Mississippi steamboats. It was made of two pieces of scrap aluminium and cost twenty cents to build.

The plan was absolutely feasible, using the air force's twin-engine B-25 Mitchell medium bomber. It could carry up to a tonne of bombs fully loaded ...

'TELL JIMMY TO GET ON HIS HORSE!'

By 1 March, a new aircraft carrier, the *Hornet*, was ready for action. Lowe went to Norfolk for another inspection tour. He wired King exultantly: 'Tell Jimmy to get on his horse!' The *Hornet* then headed for the Pacific via the Panama Canal. The new carrier and a sister carrier, *Enterprise*, would lead Task Force 16, commanded by Vice Admiral William F. Halsey. They would be supported by four cruisers and eight destroyers, plus two tankers and two submarines, with the *Enterprise* providing aerial cover. Setting out from bases at San Francisco and Pearl Harbor, the vessels were to rendezvous in the North Pacific, north of Midway Island, on the International Date Line, on 13 April.

The navy's plan called for the two carriers and four cruisers to leave the others behind on 17 April and make a high-speed dash west towards Japan. On the afternoon of 18 April, Jimmy Doolittle and his crew were to take off alone, arrive over Tokyo at dusk and drop incendiary bombs. The combustible wooden architecture of the Japanese capital would burn brightly, guiding the other fifteen planes to drop bomb loads on selected military and industrial targets in Tokyo, as well as Osaka, Nagoya and Kobe. With their mission accomplished, the big planes were then to fly one thousand kilometres into China, landing at Zhuzhou airfield. The auxiliary fuel tanks would allow them to reach Zhuzhou with twenty minutes of fuel to spare. The crews were told that if the carriers were discovered en route and came under attack by Japanese planes, they were to push the B-25s over the side to allow the *Hornet*'s own planes to be brought to the deck and sprung into action.

Things went well until early on 18 April. Then the *Enterprise*'s radar detected two Japanese picket ships sixteen kilometres ahead. Although heavy seas were breaking over the decks, the ships continued to forge ahead until a second alarm announced another

Four hours later, Doolittle was over Tokyo. Flying at 400 metres, he lined up the plane on a factory complex and told bombardier Fred Braemer to open the bomb-bay doors.

Japanese picket ship had been spotted 68 kilometres ahead. When a third picket ship was seen and radio traffic indicated that the task force had been detected, the fleet was still three hundred kilometres short of the planned launching point. Now came a stirring message from Halsey: 'To Colonel Doolittle and his gallant command. Good luck and God bless you. Halsey'.

Even though it was clear that the early takeoff meant some planes might run out of fuel before reaching safety in China, the plan was set in motion. Doolittle was first off. The carrier was pitching and tossing in the heavy seas, and the other pilots watched apprehensively as 'Colonel Jimmy' rolled down the deck. The plane passed the *Hornet*'s superstructure amidships, then, aided by a fifty-knot headwind, Doolittle eased the plane up. He made a sharp right-angle bank, and headed west. He directed the others to follow immediately. Because of the alarm sounded by the picket ships, the attack would have to be made in daylight.

By 8.20 am all were aloft, forming a ragged, low-altitude formation, then they separated as each headed for its assigned target. Four hours later, Doolittle was over Tokyo. Flying at 400 metres, he lined up over a factory complex and told bombardier Fred Braemer to open the bomb-bay doors. Braemer threw the switch on the Mark Twain bombsight and the first payback for Pearl Harbor fell on Japan.

Colonel James Doolittle aboard the *Hornet*

THE LOSSES AND THE GAINS

Initially, the Japanese were caught unawares. But soon interceptors were sent up and anti-aircraft artillery unlimbered; the guns, however, fired too high, justifying Doolittle's plan for a low-altitude sweep. In addition, the B-25s brought down more than a dozen interceptors. Ten of the U.S. bombers struck their targets. Five missed, but dropped bombs on other industrial installations, causing some damage. Only one was forced to dump its bombs short of its target. At first the Japanese declared that the 'criminal' raid had caused thousands of civilian deaths, but later announced that damage had been only minor, with few lives lost.

By military standards, the raid could not be seen as an unqualified success. In the end, all sixteen B-25s were lost, though none to enemy fire. Most ran out of fuel and crashed before reaching Zhuzhou. One plane landed in Soviet territory and the crew was interned, since the Soviet Union was not yet at war with Japan. Another crash-landed in Japan and its crew was captured and executed. On the night of 18 April, Jimmy Doolittle himself sat disconsolately in a Chinese rice paddy in Japanese-held territory, wondering if he would be court-martialled for what he feared would be a critical loss of planes and lives.

THE SILENT UNDERSEA WAR

While, in the aftermath of Pearl Harbor, aircraft carriers were the focus of planning for major offensives in the Pacific, both sides also sought to exploit their submarine fleets. The Japanese had superior undersea craft, including some with a sixteen-thousand-kilometre range—enough to reach the U.S. East Coast. But their orders were to concentrate on sinking capital ships. On 15 September 1942, off Guadalcanal, one sub sank the carrier *Wasp* and the destroyer *O'Brien* and damaged the battleship *North Carolina*. This focus on sinking warships meant they failed to cut Allied supply routes. The U.S. subs practised unrestricted warfare and focused on shipments of Japanese supplies. In the early stages, their campaign was hampered by defective torpedoes, but by 1943 new torpedoes had been introduced, which helped give the U.S. submarine fleet command of the shipping lanes.

But the Doolittle Raid had achieved many of its objectives. Material damage was not the point. Like Pearl Harbor, the attack had delivered a devastating psychological blow to the enemy's civilian population and sent a defiant message to its military command. In addition, it brought condemnation of Japan's leaders for placing the emperor's life in jeopardy (though he was unhurt, bombs fell close to his palace) and international outcry when the captured American crew was executed.

In the United States, the response to the payback raid was ecstatic, especially from Roosevelt. In a radio address he announced with tongue in cheek that the surprise attack had been launched from the Americans' secret base in 'Shangri-la'. Far from being court-martialled, Jimmy Doolittle was jumped two grades in rank, becoming a brigadier general, and was awarded the Congressional Medal of Honor. Despite the loss of planes, of the eighty men who had participated in the raid, only three, the executed prisoners, had died. Eight had been captured and five interned. Several had been badly injured and one had had a leg amputated. But most, including Doolittle, would go on to fight in other theatres of war.

The Doolittle Raid had other far-reaching effects. Before 18 April 1942, the Japanese high command had been divided on strategy. Some leaders had suggested that Japan should concentrate its offensives in the southern Pacific, protecting its conquests in Southeast Asia, and cutting the American supply route to Australia. The opposing faction, led by Admiral Isoroku Yamamoto, the architect of the Pearl Harbor attack, angrily took the Doolittle Raid as a personal affront, and advocated an offensive to knock the United States completely out of the central and northern Pacific. To kick-start this offensive, Yamamoto would later order an all-out naval attack on America's last North Pacific foothold, Midway Island—with results that were to change the course of the war.

By military standards, the raid could not be seen as an unqualified success. In the end, all sixteen B-25s were lost, though none to enemy fire.

Two Little Subs Visit Sydney

Japan's Strike at Australia

Sunday 31 May 1942 had been a pleasant, uneventful late-autumn day in Sydney. Passenger ferries crisscrossed the harbour as usual; sailboats dodged among them. The churches were full that morning; walkers and picknickers thronged the parks through the afternoon. The air raid on Darwin still preyed on people's minds; tens of thousands of Australians were fighting on the front lines in the Middle East, Europe and Asia, and the city's harbour bristled with American, British and Royal Australian Navy warships. But to Sydneysiders the war still seemed distant. Their city was at peace.

Beneath the waters of the harbour, however, a baby-faced, twenty-three-year-old Japanese naval sublieutenant was about to change all that.

NOT YOUR EVERYDAY SUBMARINE

'Nations that fear death will surely be destroyed', the sublieutenant, Katsuhisa Ban, had asserted vehemently in methodical, decorative calligraphy in a letter home a few weeks earlier. Coming from a proud Imperial Navy family, the young man was ardent in his devotion to the emperor and his homeland. As a reserve officer, he had said goodbye to his mother and younger brother as soon as war had been declared. He was immediately assigned to a midget submarine, designated *M-24*.

Midget submarines were Japan's newest weapon in the struggle for control of the world's largest ocean. The little vessels were twenty-four metres long—roughly the length of a basketball court—and one-fifth the dimension of the Imperial Navy's standard undersea craft. Inside the cramped hull, Ban could extend his arms and touch both sides.

The sub weighed 52 tonnes, was powered by a single 600-horsepower electric motor and was outfitted with two torpedo tubes and a conning tower with a hand-cranked periscope. Each torpedo carried a 450-kilogram payload. The vessel could achieve twenty-three knots on the surface, but only two knots under battery power when submerged, and thus had a range of only 160 kilometres. Because of these limitations, *M-24* had to piggyback on a mother sub. But its small size allowed it to manoeuvre into areas where larger subs could not go or would be likely to be detected. Sydney Harbour was just such a place.

Japanese sublieutenant Katsuhisa Ban

The Japanese had used midget submarines in the attack on Pearl Harbor, but with little success: they were spotted by a U.S. minesweeper and sunk by destroyers. Nevertheless, following the triumph of the aerial bombardment, the lost crewmen were venerated as 'heroes of Pearl Harbor', and Imperial Navy commander Isoruku Yamamoto continued to support the use of minisubs, despite opposition from a vocal group of admirals. In early 1942, Yamamoto was already planning an all-out attack on the U.S.'s last island bastion in the Western Pacific, at Midway. His strategy meanwhile was to knock off or disable as many warships as possible. The U.S. Navy, Royal Navy and Royal Australian Navy all used Sydney as a base for rearming and refitting ships. That placed it high on Yamamoto's list of targets.

TRAVELLING WITH MOTHER

In early May, Ban's *M-24* and other submarines began to assemble at the island of Truk in the Caroline Islands, some 2,250 kilometres north of Australia, *M-24* travelling atop its 'mother', *I-24*. Ban and his one-man crew, Petty Officer Mamoru Ashibe, underwent training while Admiral Yamamoto put the final touches to his strategy. Intelligence had told him that Australia was erecting an antisubmarine net across the mouth of Sydney Harbour, and he wanted to launch an attack before the work was completed. It was decided that three minisubs would enter Sydney Harbour. At the same time, another attack would strike the British base at Diego Suarez (now Antsiranana) in Madagascar. That two-ocean reach would show the Allies whose fleet was superior. The date picked was 31 May, like that chosen for Pearl Harbor a Sunday, when defences presumably would be down.

Ban was ready. He wrote to his family exultantly that he would drive his submarine 'into the heart of an enemy battleship'. Mounted on the mother subs, the flotilla left Truk on 18 May. Fifteen kilometres off Sydney Harbour, Ban prepared himself by praying, shaving his head, distributing his money to the sailors who had helped him get ready and writing a final farewell message. Then, on 31 May, the little subs slipped into the Tasman Sea on schedule and headed for the harbour mouth.

A series of mishaps that had begun earlier was to dog the Allied response. In the predawn hours of the day before, an unidentified float plane had circled the harbour, swooping low over the U.S. heavy cruiser *Chicago*, moored at the Garden Island naval base. A Garden Island watchman went to the *Chicago* and warned the duty officer, who brushed off the news. 'It's probably from some other U.S. ship', he said, even though no other American vessels were nearby. Another serious warning had come a few weeks earlier. The harbour floor had been laced with long electronically

The U.S. Navy, Royal Navy and Royal Australian Navy all used Sydney as a base for rearming and refitting ships. That placed it high on Yamamoto's list of targets.

sensitive cables to detect any submarines passing through. Asked to survey and analyse the new warning system, a British naval officer noted with alarm that only one man was on duty, so that the system was unmonitored during his lunch periods, bathroom breaks and sometimes at night. The British officer suggested that there should be two men on duty at all times, but his warning went unheeded.

THIRD MAN IN

Ban's *M-24* was to be the third submarine in line to enter the harbour.

M-14, commanded by Lieutenant Kenshi Chuma, went first. Only the centre section of the antisubmarine boom net had been completed, but Chuma quickly became entangled in it. Despite efforts to back off, he could not escape. An alert Maritime Services watchman, John Cargill, noticed what he termed 'a suspicious object' caught in the net and went out in a skiff to investigate. He reported it to the patrol boat *Yarroma* at 9.30 pm. An hour later, *Yarroma* received permission to drop a depth charge. It failed to destroy the sub, but five minutes after, to avoid capture, Chuma touched off the sub's demolition charge, killing himself and his crewman and destroying the vessel. The second sub, *M-21*, commanded by Lieutenant Matsuo Keiu, entered next, but was quickly spotted by two patrol boats, which illuminated it with spotlights. The patrol boat *Yandra* tried to ram the sub, then unleashed six depth charges. 'Submarine was not seen after explosion', the *Yandra* reported.

Ban was more successful. He guided *M-24* through the antisubmarine net by following in the wake of an incoming ferry, then positioned himself for attack. With few people aware of the submarine threat, the harbour remained illuminated. The bright floodlights of the Garden Island dry dock silhouetted the

The Japanese minisubmarine
M-21 being raised from
Sydney Harbour

Chicago, which had moved offshore at the news of the first sub. Viewed through Ban's periscope, and with the moon now shining brightly, the massive ship was a sitting duck. *M-24* was only 600 metres away—ideal range for a torpedo launch. Ban armed his two torpedoes and inserted them into the tubes.

The *Chicago* spotted the *M-24* and opened up with its pom-pom guns. Ban was undeterred. His sub was in a perfect firing position, and he would take advantage of it. His first torpedo missed his quarry, however, struck Garden Island and failed to explode. The second passed under the *Chicago*, thrown off course by the sub's bobbing around in the strong currents, looped under the moored Dutch submarine *X-9* and struck the seawall behind the *Kuttabul*, a former ferry that had been converted into a naval supply and depot vessel and was now used as a dormitory. The blast tore a huge hole in the *Kuttabul*. Twenty-one men died and ten others were wounded.

A BELATED RESPONSE

The explosion galvanised the harbour into a belated response. The warships and the *X-9* quickly put to sea, while other navy craft searched the harbour for traces of the elusive *M-24*. Ferry traffic was suspended, ships' running lights were extinguished and the

FOUND AT LAST

When the first two minisubs were located, lifted to the surface, and put on display across Australia, it was assumed that Ban's *M-24* had escaped the harbour, sunk or been scuttled offshore. But sixty-four years later, in 2006, a group of amateur divers located the wreck in about fifty metres of water off Long Reef, near Sydney's Northern Beaches. The sunken sub was videotaped and the film shown on television; meanwhile, the Japanese and Australian governments discussed whether to raise it, open it in place to look for bodies and to hold services for Ban and Ashibe. At the time of writing, no decision had yet been taken.

Garden Island dry dock went dark. No trace of the *M-24* could be found, however, and the search was called off at daylight. Sydney nervously went back to bed. Offshore, the three larger subs waited for the midgets to reappear, but after a day and a half withdrew. Nine days later, submarines returned, shelling Sydney's eastern suburbs and the coastal city of Newcastle, and leading some residents to move inland, out of the danger zone. There were no further submarine attacks in southeastern Australia, but attacks, mostly by air, continued against Darwin in the north.

M-21 and *M-14* were raised from the depths, but Ban's submarine was presumed lost. The bodies of the four crewmen that could be found were cremated and then buried with full military honours—despite protests, Rear Admiral G.C. Muirhead-Gould, in charge of Sydney's harbour defences, insisted that the men were patriots deserving of such a tribute. Besides, he hoped that his chivalrous treatment might impress on the Japanese how combatants should be treated—a critical point in the wake of the Bataan Death March and alleged atrocities against Australians after the fall of Singapore. The ashes of the crewmen were returned to Japan via the neutral Swiss consulate. In Japan, all four were acclaimed 'Hero Gods', and posthumously promoted two ranks. Katsuhisa Ban, the man who courted heroic death, became a full commander.

An Alaskan Diversion

The Japanese Occupation of the Aleutian Islands

The island of Attu would qualify for any list of the bleakest, most forlorn places on Earth. Just 56 kilometres long and 32 wide, it lies at the westernmost extremity of the Aleutian Island chain and is therefore part of Alaska and the United States; yet it is 18,000 kilometres from the Alaskan mainland and nearly 4000 kilometres as the crow flies from the U.S. mainland. Its nearest neighbour is Siberia, some 55 kilometres across an unruly channel between the Pacific Ocean and the Bering Sea.

It rains on Attu. It rains and rains, five days out of every seven. When it's not raining, it's often snowing. Six days of clear skies a year is a lot. The winds often blow at 160 kilometres per hour and can be so strong that a man could lean into them at a forty-five-degree angle and be supported. There are no trees or shrubs. The island's terrain of steep hills, some up to 900 metres high, with deep intertwining valleys, are carpeted with muskeg—a spongy, semifrozen layer of compacted moss, lichens and tundra that can be as much as one metre thick and has a fragile crust. In places, a man can step into it and sink up to his knees. Only a few hardy flowers grow on the island, and you have to look closely to find them amid the mottled green and brown of the muskeg. Like most of the far north, Attu has long winter nights and short winter days. Not that the sun is seen much, regardless of the season. Normally, it is hidden behind a deep, impenetrable blanket of fog.

In 1942, Attu was inhabited by a small community of forty-eight native Aleut people. The Aleuts are closely related to the Siberians, ethnically and linguistically, and, indeed, are thought to

U.S. troops firing a howitzer on Attu

have arrived in the Aleutian Islands from Siberia, by way of a land bridge between the two continents, about twenty-five thousand years ago. The Aleut community on Attu was governed by elders and administered by a first chief. It eked out a meagre existence from the sea, the men heading out in sealskin boats to haul in salmon, cod or halibut for salting and drying, and hunting seals, sea lions and otters for skins and meat. They dressed in furs, skin side out to protect against the unceasing rain, and ate a diet heavy on protein and fat. Alongside the Aleuts lived, it was said, only 'a few blue foxes'—and two hardy Americans.

Etta Jones, sixty-two, and her husband, C. Foster Jones, had migrated from the Lower Forty-eight in October 1941, two months before the Japanese attack on Pearl Harbor, in the spirit of pioneers. Foster was a radio technician and short-wave ham, and an amateur weather observer who sent daily weather readings to the U.S. military installation at Dutch Harbor, on the island of Unalaska, thirteen hundred kilometres east along the archipelago. Etta taught a handful of native Aleut children in a Bureau of Indian Affairs (BIA) school in Chichagof, a cluster of small frame houses and semi-subterranean dwellings carved into the muskeg. She was a dedicated teacher who had also trained as a nurse. Etta thought Attu wild and lovely, and she was to spend four years longing for it while she remained in exile and Americans fought one of the most tenacious and vicious battles of the war to regain it.

Like most of the far north, Attu has long winter nights and short winter days. Not that the sun is seen much, regardless of the season.

THE WAR COMES TO ATTU

Occasionally, boats would visit Attu to trade for fish or skins, bringing other foodstuffs. Missionaries arrived infrequently, as did government patrol boats and a BIA boat bringing mail. Otherwise, Foster Jones's radio was the only link with the outside world. In December, it brought news of the Pearl Harbor attack.

On paper, this meant that Attu was at war with Japan, its 'near' neighbour; but Pearl Harbor was 3,200 kilometres away and little more than a name, and the Aleuts were somewhat familiar with the Japanese, whose fishing boats often ventured north in quest of the wily salmon. 'War' had little meaning to people who had never experienced it and whose chief enemies were the gods of weather. Aside from the Joneses, no one on Attu had ever seen an aeroplane; they probably couldn't have, anyway, because of the everlasting fog.

But then, on 3 June 1942, Jones's radio crackled with further news. Japanese planes operating from carriers had bombed Dutch Harbor that morning. Swooping out of a heavily overcast sky, expecting to find a carrier fleet in port, they had been surprised to find an empty harbour, but had then dumped their bombs on a naval barracks, killing twenty-five sailors and wounding twenty-five others.

Two days later, on 5 June, the Joneses looked out of their cabin and saw a transport ship anchored offshore. This seemed like good news. For days, the talk on the radio had been about U.S. plans to evacuate the Aleutians and this vessel was no doubt their means of deliverance. But then they heard rifle shots and heard yelling in a strange language. Outside, Japanese soldiers came running over the muskeg towards their building. Jones sent one final message to Dutch Harbor and then went outside, hands upraised in surrender. A Japanese officer, shouting in English, pushed past him and entered. He poked a bayonet at Etta. 'How many are you?' he shouted. 'Two', she replied coolly, then, 'How many are you?' 'Two thousand!' the officer declared. He was off by several hundred. By nightfall, the transport had landed 2,700 troops, who took control of the island. They stripped it of its human population and dug in to establish a bastion from which they might attack—or at least intimidate—the United States.

As soon as he had stepped outside, Jones had been taken into custody and away from Etta's sight. She herself was questioned three times but finally released when the Japanese concluded she had no military information. On 12 June, she found herself aboard a freighter with the rest of Attu's Aleut population, headed for Japan.

A CASE OF DECEPTION

Originally, the landing in the Aleutians, carried out by only a small force, was meant to trick the Americans into believing the main force might strike there rather than at Midway. But on 4 June, the Imperial Navy was struck a devastating blow. Intelligence had told the Americans that the Japanese fleet was headed for Midway, and that day an American naval dive-bomber squadron came across the Japanese aircraft carriers while their planes were on deck refuelling. The U.S. force quickly destroyed four carriers, along with 300 planes. Humiliated (the Japanese people were never told of the defeat), the Japanese high command decided

WHERE DID EVERYONE GO?

After retaking Attu, the Americans zeroed in on the more redoubtable Kiska. They put together an enormous invasion force, consisting of 34,000 ground troops, 5,500 of them Canadian, plus an armada of fifty warships, led by three battleships, one light cruiser and nineteen destroyers. The air force consisted of more than one hundred heavy, medium and dive-bombers, and sixty fighters. After bombing the island for two weeks, and even dropping leaflets calling on the Japanese to surrender, the invasion force went ashore on 15 August. Unknown to them, however, on 27 July, under cover of heavy fog, the entire Japanese force had slipped away, taking its equipment with it, lock, stock and barrel. It took four days for the invading force to realise this. In the meantime, the Americans and Canadians blundered around in the fog, shooting at anything that moved and often at each other. More than three hundred Americans were wounded, and seventeen Americans and four Canadians killed—all by friendly fire.

it was important to pursue its 'diversionary' Aleutian campaign for psychological and propaganda reasons. So, it beefed up the Attu force and also took over the island of Kiska, 50 kilometres to the east, which had a better harbour and less forbidding terrain. There they captured another U.S. weather station and the ten sailors who manned it.

Despite the islands' distance from the heartland and lack of strategic significance, the United States was genuinely alarmed by the loss of territory. Miniscule though they were, these islands had to be recovered, as a matter of honour, and their inhabitants protected. The government vowed to replant the U.S. flag on the far-off outpost as soon as possible.

Meanwhile, Etta and the captured Aleuts arrived in Yokohama on 21 June, having travelled together in the hold of the ship, sleeping on the floor. At Yokohama, Etta was separated from the others. Together with eighteen Australian nurses who had been captured in New Guinea, she was transferred to Yokohama's Bund Hotel, where she was again interrogated, and then to the Yokohama Athletic and Rowing Club and finally to a prison camp at Yokosuka, thirty kilometres from Tokyo. For her, it was a far cry from Attu. Though she had lived on that remote outpost for only eight months, she had come to love its wild land and, especially, her little Aleutian students.

BOUNCING DOWN THE RUNWAY

Over the next year, both the Japanese and the Americans struggled to make headway in the Aleutians. Neither side had truly reckoned on the atrocious weather and hostile environment. Unable to land their earthmoving equipment in Attu's rocky harbour, the Japanese tried to carve out a landing strip using manpower and shovels, then gave up and focused their efforts on Kiska. There they were more successful, though the few

Despite the islands' distance from the heartland and lack of strategic significance, the United States was genuinely alarmed by the loss of territory.

vehicles brought ashore at Kiska quickly sank, wheels spinning, into the muskeg. Ships bringing supplies and reinforcements repeatedly collided in the unceasing fog.

The Americans built an airstrip on another island, Adak, by laying a metal mesh strip across the bouncy muskeg. One pilot compared it to 'trying to land on an innerspring mattress'. Warships shelling Japanese positions were forced to fire blind, unable to see their targets through the fog. Flyers had the same problem. When the Adak landing strip proved less than satisfactory as a springboard for dive-bombers, the U.S. Air Force turned to flying heavy, long-range bombers from the Alaskan mainland. But the Flying Fortresses were seldom able to see their targets on Attu and Kiska and simply dropped their bombs and hoped for the best. The Japanese, meanwhile, flying from their makeshift runway on Kiska, staged retaliatory bombing runs on Dutch Harbor.

Finally, the U.S. high command decided enough was enough. Bypassing Kiska, the stronger of the two Japanese installations, on 11 May 1943, they put the Seventh Infantry Division ashore and backed them up with a heavy naval bombardment. The strategy called for half the force to land on the island's north side, half on the south; the two halves would then unite at the island's central ridge and sweep the island from one end to the other. The landing party anticipated a Japanese force of five hundred; instead, it ran into nearly three thousand Japanese troops, who fought tenaciously for every bit of ground.

It was expected the battle would be over in five days; it took nineteen.

The Americans were hampered by faulty intelligence. They had no maps and only one outdated Coast and Geodetic Survey of the coastline. The men had trained for the landing on the sandy beaches of California and were ill prepared for Attu, where their assault boats could not make it ashore in the rocky harbour and

Surprised at first by the ferocity of the two-directional attack, the Japanese soon occupied the high ground and poured a withering fire down on the Americans.

the men were forced to wade in icy water up to their thighs. They arrived in classic winter uniforms of field jackets, wool trousers and leather boots, ill suited to the miserable conditions and minus four-degree Celsius temperatures. Ultimately, trench foot, frostbite and exposure accounted for far more casualties than enemy bullets. Three hundred men had to have feet amputated.

The fighting quickly degenerated into bloody, hand-to-hand struggles. Surprised at first by the ferocity of the two-directional attack, the Japanese soon occupied the high ground and poured a withering fire down on the Americans. The infantrymen found it almost impossible to dig foxholes in the muskeg to protect themselves. The Japanese used novel tactics neither the planners nor the assaulting troops had experienced before; for example, from the heights, they simply rolled grenades down at the Americans. Finally, one Seventh Division infantryman, Private George Mirich, could stand it no longer. Despite a hail of fire that crippled one arm, he advanced to the ridgetop thereafter known as Bloody Point, and shot, one by one, the defending Japanese, then used his rifle as a club against the others until they withdrew, yielding the commanding position to the invaders and turning the tide towards the Americans.

On 17 May, the Americans, resting and solidifying their control of the lower ground, met another frightening and unfamiliar tactic: the banzai charge. Charging towards the Americans while screaming and firing their rifles wildly, the Japanese took back much of the ground lost previously, before the Americans recovered and met them with withering machine-gun fire. Yet the Japanese kept coming, seemingly courting death, throwing grenades, but also holding them against their own chests and committing suicide as they ran. When the battle for Attu ended, only eighteen Japanese were taken prisoner. The Americans counted more than 2300 corpses and were sure there were more buried in the muskeg by the bombardments. The United States suffered 3,829 casualties—nearly one-quarter of the invading force. Of these, 549 were killed and 1,148 wounded. More than 1,900 were hospitalised with severe cold injuries or disease. On 30 May 1943, 'the lonesomest spot this side of Hell', as one soldier called it, was in American hands.

'THE AGED ONE'

At the prison camp in Yokosuka, Etta and her companions were treated with respect, she recalled later. Guards addressed her as *Oba San*, 'the aged one', which she took as a sign of politeness and respect. She spent much of her time in needlework, making small cloth bags which the Japanese purchased for a few cents to hold their religious pictures.

The Aleuts fared less well. They were ordered to work in the Otaru dolomite mines on the island of Hokkaido, and, although the work was not arduous and they were paid a small amount, they were often beaten and told to work harder. The traditional Aleut social structure broke down. The abrupt change from their traditional meat-and-fish diet brought disastrous results, weakening the captives and contributing to deaths from illness, notably tuberculosis. Of the forty-five Attu natives who were taken to Japan, only twenty-eight survived.

Etta Jones never returned to Attu, never saw her husband again and was never able to learn what had happened to him. One rumour said he had committed suicide in custody, another that he had been shot by the Japanese as a spy because of his knowledge of radio. Etta was repatriated to the United States by plane on 1 September 1945, after the Japanese surrender. Waiting for her was a BIA cheque, for $7,371 in back pay.

A Disastrous Dress Rehearsal

The Allied Raid on Dieppe

On a typical, prewar August day, the pebbly beach in front of the Dieppe casino, on France's Normandy coast, would have been bathed in sunshine and carpeted with tanning bodies. Laughing children would have been splashing in the lapping surf while their mothers sat under beach umbrellas and sipped lemonade. Sailing dinghies would have been tacking offshore, young men tossing balls on the beach. But on this August day—19 August 1942—the scene was far from such an idyll. The pebbles were covered with bodies, but they were the bodies of Canadian soldiers: dead, dying, wounded or frightened into immobility. Overhead rattled the fire of machine guns and the *whoomf!* of mortars, keeping the men pinned to the pebbles. Planes swooped and dived at each other, some falling into the sea in flames. Warships offshore added to the din with their guns; artillery onshore responded, their shells exploding in the water.

Across the beach, under the enfilading fire, darted a solitary figure. He hurried from man to fallen man, comforting, offering water and praying with those bleeding and near death. He stopped, lifting a man onto his back, hustled with him to a makeshift hospital, then returned for another. Although he wore a uniform and a Red Cross armband, John Weir Foote was not a medic, but a minister. Nevertheless, he was about to become a hero, on the most disastrous day in Canadian military history.

A smash across the Channel into Hitler's Fortress Europe would obviously please everyone, and a vast army was being massed in Britain to jump off into France.

German troops with a captured Canadian tank, after the failed raid on Dieppe

AN INVASION IN MINIATURE

In mid-1942, the British high command began to look again at the idea of a land invasion of mainland Europe. Churchill's new, eager-beaver Chief of Combined Operations, Lord Louis Mountbatten, was thirsting for action. A smash across the Channel into Hitler's Fortress Europe would obviously please everyone, and a vast army was being massed in Britain to jump off into France. But political and military strategists alike agreed that the burgeoning force was green, and by no means ready for all-out combat. And too many questions had to be answered before an invasion could take place. Would it be better to hammer German strongholds straight on, or to first establish bridgeheads on the beaches, land more troops, and expand from there? Could air, naval and ground forces collaborate on the scale an invasion of such scope would demand? Should the first target be a French seaport that could be converted to a supply depot for incoming manpower and personnel?

Gradually, it dawned on the strategists that the best way to answer these questions might be to test the plan on a small scale. An invasion in miniature could be mounted, using limited forces but the same detailed planning and surprise that would be required for a large-scale invasion. Such an operation might disclose the enemy's defensive strategy and how the Germans would react to such an attack—would they, for example, bring in troops from Russia to bolster the Atlantic defences? A quick victory might also give the Allies a psychological and propaganda boost. And it might please the anxious Stalin.

Canadian troops had been stewing restlessly in Britain since the fall of France. Many of them were seasoned veterans of the 1940 campaigns, anxious for another go at the Germans. The Canadian commander, Andrew McNaughton, wanted his men to gain some combat experience after two years of inactivity. Thus, Mountbatten tapped the Canadian Second Division to lead the raid, or rather to carry out the prearranged plan, in which they had had little voice.

After much consideration, Dieppe was chosen as the target. From the planners' point of view, it had many advantages. It lay only 40 kilometres from the British coast, within easy range of RAF bases and allowing a quick thrust across the Channel and an equally quick return home. It was one of the safest ports on the Channel, and suitable for the kinds of vessels that would be needed in an invasion build-up. The city sat on a promontory overlooking its harbour; directly below, in front of the casino, was a pebble beach and on either side of it were two wide sand beaches ideal for amphibious landings. Headlands at the ends of the sand beaches commanded the waterfront.

The strategists insistently used the term 'raid' for the attack, named Operation Jubilee, to emphasise that a brief foray was planned, not a long-term campaign; but they drafted a plan that was complex—perhaps too complex, as critics were to charge later. Two teams of one hundred British commandos would land before dawn, climb the headlands and silence the artillery mounted there. With the first wisps of daylight would come a two-pronged flank attack on the east and west beaches, with the crack Royal Regiment of Canada tackling the eastern strip of sand, and the Queen's Own Cameron Highlanders from Winnipeg and the South Saskatchewan Regiment the west. Half an hour later, the main thrust would be directed at the pebble beach in front of the old casino, clearing the way for the landing of tanks. Here, the attackers would be the Essex Scottish Regiment from western Ontario, on the eastern kilometre of the pebble beach, called Red Beach; and on the western kilometres, or White Beach, the Royal Hamilton Light Infantry, also from Ontario. The RHLI's chaplain was Honorary Captain John Weir Foote.

THE CHAPLAIN'S MISSION

Foote was thirty-eight years old, a Presbyterian minister who had held pastorates in Quebec and Ontario. When the war began, he decided his ministerial mission lay with the troops: men under fire would need spiritual guidance more than those safely at home. He left his pulpit and volunteered for the Canadian Chaplain's Service, which assigned him as regimental chaplain to the Wentworth Regiment of the RHLI. Named an honorary captain, he was sent to France too late for the 1940 campaigns. When he heard hints about Operation Jubilee, he went to the RHLI commanding officer, Lieutenant Colonel Robert Ridley Labatt. 'I know what's in the wind, Bob', he said. 'I want to go.' Labatt refused, so Foote rejoined, 'Then I'll make my own arrangements. If you should see me on the beaches, you can order me off'. Labatt relented, agreeing to list Foote as a litter carrier attached to the regimental field hospital.

An important part of Operation Jubilee, the generals agreed, was to maintain absolute secrecy, as in an eventual invasion. They would move in total darkness, with radios turned off until they were close to shore. There would be no preliminary bombardment, either from the sea or from the air, to alert the German defences that an attack was coming.

Thus, just after midnight on 19 August, boats slipped away from the ports of Southampton, Portsmouth, Shoreham and Newhaven carrying the 5000 Canadians, 200 British commandos, and fifty U.S. Rangers. They were escorted by a cruiser, destroyers

> They were escorted by a cruiser, destroyers and minesweepers, and backed up by RAF squadrons ready to lay smokescreens and provide aerial cover for the landings.

and minesweepers, and backed up by RAF squadrons ready to lay smokescreens and provide aerial cover for the landings. The armada totalled 240 ships, and was 3 kilometres wide and 8 deep.

Everything was going according to plan at 3 am. The infantrymen, including Honorary Captain Foote, were loaded into shallow-draught assault boats for the amphibious landing. But then, as they approached France, a lookout noticed the silhouette of a convoy moving slowly along the coast. Almost simultaneously, a star shell illuminated the sky as the convoy spotted the British vessels. A brief exchange of gunfire occurred, with minor damage on both sides. One German vessel was able to notify the shoreline defenders. Operation Jubilee's cover was blown.

NO TURNING BACK

Having lost the element of surprise, some commanders wanted to turn back, but they were overridden. The operation was to go ahead as scheduled. At 4.25 am, the commando teams were to be landed to strike the coastal batteries. The team assigned to the western battery succeeded in its mission. But Commando Team 3 had been scattered by the sea fight and many of its boats never reached shore. Those who did were overwhelmed by a storm of fire. It was an ominous start.

At 4.52 am, the two flanking attacks were launched, too, and were immediately pinned down. On the eastern flank, later described as 'an abattoir', the men of the Royal Regiment, having lost the advantages of surprise and darkness, were met as they stepped out of their landing craft by a storm of machine-gun and mortar fire. Bullets and shrapnel cut them down in waves, far from the headland they were supposed to attack. In the west, where Commando Team 4 had silenced the coastal battery, the South Saskatchewan Regiment and the Cameron Highlanders landed successfully and reached the town of Dieppe and an airfield beyond. But then they were halted by heavy fire and savaged as they attempted to withdraw to the beach.

On schedule at 5.20 am, the main assault force, led by the Royal Hamiltons, hit the pebble beach. It, too, was pinned down by machine-gun fire, with one RHLI company virtually wiped out right at the shoreline. Others tried to take shelter behind a seawall, but it left little protection against deadly fire raking the position from the flank.

Another company managed to reach the town and fight a close-in battle for the casino—with tragic results. General McNaughton had held the French Canadian Fusiliers Mont-Royal from Quebec offshore in reserve, to be sent in to clinch a successful landing. When a radio message stated that the casino had been captured, he interpreted that to mean that victory was imminent. So he sent the Fusiliers in, and they were similarly pinned down by snipers and devastated. The commanders sent an SOS to the RAF for support, but the Spitfires and Hurricanes were quickly met by German fighters and bombers, and one of the most disastrous and one-sided aerial combats of the war resulted. The RAF lost 106 planes, the Luftwaffe only 48.

A MAKESHIFT HOSPITAL

On the pebble beach, Chaplain Foote had his hands full. A blasted tank landing craft had been marooned on the beach by the ebb tide, and wounded, frightened men were huddling in its shelter, where doctors, medical personnel and litter bearers had improvised a regimental aid station. Foote could also see many wounded men lying exposed on the beach, unable or afraid to crawl to the shelter under the unceasing mortar and machine-gun fire. They had to be helped, he thought. Disregarding the danger, he hunched over, zigzagged to the nearest one, hoisted him on his shoulders and staggered back to the shelter. Then he ventured

Canadian soldiers returning
from Dieppe

out to save another, and another. Over the next two hours, he brought in twenty-eight men, some of them severely wounded. It was a dispiriting and tiring duty, even for one of his size and strength, for sometimes he had to pass up a man in the agonies of death in order to help someone more likely to survive.

The bold 'raid' had become a disaster. Canada's proudest units had been decimated; the Royal Regiment Guards had suffered ninety per cent casualties. No course of action remained but withdrawal. But that also meant reassembling the ships that had been dispersed to await the end of the mission, and many of the wooden landing craft that could transfer men to the larger boats offshore had been shattered or sunk. At 9.30 therefore, McNaughton ordered the evacuation to begin at 11 am. That would give the men time to gather the boats; but it also meant many more would die before the rescue effort commenced.

TRY AND TRY AGAIN

With neither side making a breakthrough, both Allied and Axis powers strove to develop weapons that would overwhelm their opponents. A month after Dieppe, the so-called 'Manhattan Project' began in the United States, which aimed to create an atomic bomb by harnessing the power of a neutron chain reaction in a form of uranium, a process known as nuclear fission. The Germans were attempting something similar, but using a different method, employing heavy water. Their only reliable source of heavy water was the Norsk Hydro Plant at Rjuken in Norway. Having realised this, Britain's Special Operations Executive determined to destroy it. Following reconnaissance, the British sent gliders full of commandos to attack the plant, but the operation fell apart when two gliders crashed, killing thirty-four men. In February 1943, Norwegian commandos on skis crept into the plant, planted explosive charges, then skied 400 kilometres to Sweden. The explosives disabled the station for several months, but it was rebuilt. American B-17s then bombed the plant; they caused only minor damage, but it was enough to convince the Nazis to move the stocks of heavy water to Germany by boat. A Norwegian commando planted a timed plastic explosive in the boat's hold, sinking the boat and bringing Germany's nuclear program to an end.

'I MUST STAY WITH THEM'

Desperate men were already gathering well before 11 am, only to be cut down by German fire. Foote watched, horrified, as men stripped off their clothes and plunged into the water, hoping to swim to the larger ships or even to England—almost impossible, but trying was better than death on a strange, blood-soaked beach. When the boats arrived, men scrambled over each other to pile in, swamping the boats and overturning them.

Foote now began a different rescue effort. It was one thing for otherwise healthy men to reach the boats and be taken to safety, he thought to himself, but the wounded had to be helped, too. He wearily lifted a disabled man to his shoulders. 'Each man carry a man!' he shouted and trudged towards the water. As the boats were loaded, he carried another thirty men from the makeshift hospital to the waterfront and safety. He became soaked to the skin, and his boots waterlogged and heavy; he stripped them off and continued barefoot. As the last boat was loading, those who had witnessed his heroic actions grabbed his arms and yanked him into the boat. The boat pushed away, leaving others still on the beach. Foote suddenly stood up and said, 'I must stay with them'. Then he leaped overboard, waded ashore and walked towards the German lines, where he was forced to walk, bootless, through the cinders along railway tracks. He would subsequently be sent to a prison camp and remain there for the rest of the war before returning to Canada, a Victoria Cross and a successful career in the Ontario parliament and several government positions.

The final tally for the seven-hour dress rehearsal was 907 killed, 600 seriously wounded, and 1900 taken prisoner. Sixty-eight per cent of the landing force had become casualties. The commanders assessed the outcome and declared that many important lessons had been learned. The enemy, they acknowledged, might well have learned some, too.

'A German Field Marshal Never Surrenders'

The Siege of Stalingrad

Many a German male named Friedrich has had his name shortened to the traditional familiar form 'Fritz', but nobody ever dared do that to General Friedrich Paulus, commander of the German Sixth Army. Probably not even his trophy wife, a Romanian noblewoman who gloried in her own nickname, 'Coco', would have taken such improprieties. A strikingly handsome fifty-two-year-old with the erect bearing of the professional soldier, Paulus lived by an iron code of proper behaviour, courtesy and military discipline. Fastidious to a fault, he bathed and changed uniforms twice a day and unfailingly wore gloves in the field—he was phobic about dirt. He followed orders without question and expected his own commands to be carried out to the letter.

The son of a bookkeeper, Paulus had been rejected as a naval cadet, left law school after one year and enrolled as an army officer candidate in time for World War I, eventually achieving the rank of captain. After the Armistice, he was assigned to the army planning office, where he became known for toying with sandbox battlefield models. He became an ardent champion of the Nazi regime, seeing Hitlerism as the answer to German's post-war woes. The Führer himself was a military genius, in Paulus's eyes, outthinking and outstrategising the traditionalists on the general staff. Hitler returned the compliment. He found Paulus a kindred spirit because he, like Hitler, came from a modest background.

He was not one of those monocled snobs from the aristocratic Prussian hierarchy who dominated military headquarters. He and Paulus understood each other.

Or so they thought. In fact, their failure to understand each other would lead to one of the most catastrophic German losses of the war, the deaths of hundreds of thousands of men and a major shift of fortune in favour of the Allies.

THE FÜHRER'S FAVOURITE

There were those who had misgivings about the relationship. General Heinz Guderian, architect of the blitzkrieg that had overwhelmed Poland, found Paulus 'brilliantly clever, conscientious, hard-working, original and talented', but doubted his toughness. Coco detested Hitler and told her husband he was too good for the 'lackeys' serving the Nazi regime.

By 1941, Paulus had established himself as such a favourite that Hitler personally dispatched him to North Africa to quell his old colleague Rommel. Having driven the British back, Rommel wanted to mount a major offensive on the Suez Canal; but Hitler wanted to save the troops for Operation Barbarossa, his coming invasion of the Soviet Union. Paulus carried out his instructions faithfully and a reluctant Rommel obeyed. Paulus went home, was promoted to lieutenant general and appointed deputy chief of the general staff. He thereupon threw himself into the detailed planning of Barbarossa. Prophetically, when he brought the plans home, Coco was appalled—and frightened. 'What will become of us all?' she cried. 'Who will survive to the end?'

The fastidious General Friedrich Paulus

When German troops crossed the Soviet border on 22 June 1941, Paulus quit planning and became second in command of the Sixth Army. In January 1942, his superior, Field Marshal Walther von Reichenau, died suddenly, and he moved up to commanding general. He was not a unanimous choice. Others on the general staff complained of his lack of experience and agreed with Guderian about his indecisiveness; Paulus, the grumblers said, wouldn't move until he was sure he had planned for every possible detail. To mollify the critics, Hitler appointed the more aggressive General Arthur Schmidt as Paulus's deputy.

OPERATION BLUE

Paulus and Schmidt's Sixth Army, with 250,000 men, 500 tanks and 7,000 guns and mortars, was to be part of Army Group South, consisting also of the Sixteenth Army and two panzer corps. Army Group South was to drive across and conquer the Ukraine, Russia's breadbasket and industrial heartland, and eventually capture the oilfields of the Caucasus. Oil was critical to the heavily mechanised, petrol-guzzling German tanks and aircraft.

Paulus partly overcame his reluctant-warrior reputation in 'Operation Blue', the code name for the Caucasus campaign. In late May and June 1942, Army Group South encircled the Soviet defenders at Kharkov and crushed them, taking 239,000 prisoners and capturing 1,240 sorely needed tanks. 'The great thing now', Paulus exultantly wrote home, 'is to hit the Russian so hard a crack that he won't recover for a very long time'. But as Paulus readied himself for a renewed drive on the Caucasus, Hitler changed his mind. The original plan for Operation Blue was to bypass the city of Stalingrad, a major population and industrial city on the Volga River, where many of the Soviet tanks and vehicles were built. Hitler realised it was not smart strategy or tactics to leave such a large and potentially threatening strongpoint in your rear. Besides,

> ... the Germans could envelop the huge Russian army before it could retreat into Stalingrad. Such a masterstroke might even end the war, right there.

taking a city named for the Soviet leader would have immense propaganda value. So Paulus was ordered to attack Stalingrad.

Paulus obeyed unquestioningly, moving his troops into the vast steppes north of the city. Then a golden opportunity opened for the German armies. General Hermann 'Papa' Hoth's Second Army outflanked the Soviet Sixty-fourth Army and reached the railway leading to Stalingrad, just thirty kilometres west of the city. If the Sixth Army could quickly drive south to meet him, Hoth told the general staff, the Germans could envelop the huge Russian army before it could retreat into Stalingrad. Such a masterstroke might even end the war, right there. But, living up to his reputation, Paulus protested that his troops were not ready and asked for a few days to prepare. By the time he decided that everything was in place, on 3 September, it was too late. The Soviet armies had withdrawn into Stalingrad, where German tanks could not easily manoeuvre and fighting fell to infantrymen on foot.

The Luftwaffe launched a massive bombardment that largely turned the city to rubble. The Sixty-second Army under Vasily Chuikov took up positions on rooftops and in ruined factories, hotels, shops and apartments. The Germans faced cleverly camouflaged artillery and machine-gun nests and pinpoint snipers. The Soviet defenders were tenacious, fighting block by block, building by building, floor by floor, room by room, staircase by staircase. 'We have taken the kitchen', one German soldier cracked. 'Now we must fight for the living room.' As the Soviets were pushed back towards the Volga, they even retreated into the sewers and fought there. Men battled with knives, clubs, shovels, even rocks. Chuikov ordered his men to 'hug' the enemy—stay close and fight hand to hand. That way, the Germans would hesitate to call in artillery or an airstrike for fear of hitting their own men. The Germans called this type of fighting Rattenkrieg, 'war of the rats'.

German soldiers advancing
warily through a decimated
factory during the battle
for Stalingrad

NO FREEDOM OF ACTION

This was a kind of war Paulus had not depicted in his sandbox models. He was losing men by the thousands. By 1 November 1942, he held ninety per cent of the city and the swastika flew over Red Square, yet the Russians were still fighting and, indeed, bringing reinforcements across the Volga at night. Temperatures were dropping, snow was falling. Paulus's appeals for more troops, fuel and ammunition were falling on deaf ears. And it was all taking a toll on him personally: the imperturbable general developed an uncontrollable tic in his right eye. He began to keep to himself, leaving combat decisions to Schmidt.

By 19 November, the Germans seemed to have the upper hand. But then the Soviets struck back. The legendary Marshal Georgy Zhukov took command of Russian forces, assembled three armies of nearly a million men and threw them around the city. Now it was the Germans who were encircled and cut off from supplies.

A very worried Paulus asked for the Führer's permission to try to break out of the trap, while he still had the resources. No way, Hitler replied, 'No power on earth will force us out of Stalingrad'. A week later, Paulus tried again. His tanks were almost empty of fuel, his troops almost out of rations, ammunition was scarce. The Hungarian, Romanian, Croatian and Italian troops protecting his flanks were almost mutinous. His own officers were declaring a breakout attempt was the army's only chance. He implored for 'freedom of action', which Hitler took to mean permission to retreat or surrender. Ignoring his top advisers, who wanted to save the Sixth Army to fight another day, the Führer replied, 'The Sixth Army will hold its position despite the threat of encirclement', ignoring the fact that encirclement had already occurred.

Aside from saving face, Hitler had a sound strategic reason for wanting to cling to Stalingrad at all costs. Field Marshal Ewald von Kleist's armies had reached the shores of the Caspian Sea and the key oil port of Baku, but had been forced to withdraw by winter weather and overextended supply lines. Hitler hoped to hold Stalingrad long enough for Paulus and Kleist to unite and launch a renewed offensive on the oilfields. Retaining Stalingrad was crucial to that plan.

Hitler glibly promised that Göring's vaunted Luftwaffe would supply the beleaguered garrison by air. Paulus said that would require air-dropping over six hundred tonnes of supplies a day. What? Hitler said. How about three hundred? How about quadrupling the twenty to thirty planes now dropping supplies? But over the next month even that meagre quota was reached only three times. The planes simply were not available and those available were constantly grounded by the vicious weather.

Paulus was forced to cut rations by a third, then cut them again. By 12 December, one loaf of bread was being shared by five men. At Christmas, a few forlorn men fashioned 'Christmas trees' out of scraps of wood and waveringly sang carols. Their Christmas 'dinner' was a single slice of bread and a cup of watery soup. 'The horses have been eaten', one man wrote home. 'I would eat a cat. I have heard their flesh is very tasty.'

TO THE LAST MAN

'Manstein is coming! Manstein is coming!' In mid-December, this cry ran through the Sixth Army. Field Marshal Erich von Manstein was known as a soldier's soldier, and widely admired in the ranks. Earlier, at Hitler's behest, he had airlifted his intelligence officer into Stalingrad to assess Paulus's plight. Manstein reported back that Paulus's army was on the point of collapse, and suggested that he should lead a relief column to save Stalingrad. Hitler approved. When word reached Stalingrad, the men were ecstatic, overwhelmed with relief that they might be rescued from their hellish plight. By 19 December, Manstein and his tanks were

... the Führer replied, 'The Sixth Army will hold its position despite the threat of encirclement', ignoring the fact that encirclement had already occurred.

within fifty kilometres of the city; the besieged garrison could hear the boom of his guns. But then a giant snowstorm bogged down the relief column and Manstein abandoned the rescue, leaving Paulus on his own.

On 8 January, the Russian general Rokossovsky messaged Paulus under a flag of truce. As 'the cruel Russian winter has only just begun', now was the time to surrender, he said. Paulus dutifully passed the demand on to Hitler, who again responded, 'Surrender is forbidden. Sixth Army will hold their position to the last man and the last round'. Paulus remained steadfast, but his deputy, General Schmidt, laughed hollowly. His men didn't have a last round to fire if they wanted to. Men were freezing to death while they slept and dying of untreated wounds. Seeing no way out, five Italian soldiers went out into the bitter, minus-thirty-degree cold and committed suicide by freezing to death, sitting side by side.

> 'He put the pistol in Paulus's hand', one observer said; in other words, Hitler had given him no honourable course other than suicide.

THE ONLY WAY OUT?

With a few planes and the single landing strip still accessible, the Germans began to evacuate wounded and key personnel, technicians and selected commanders. As each plane prepared to take off, panicky men mobbed it, the healthier trampling the weaker and trying to cling to the plane as it lifted into the air.

No evacuation order came, however. Instead, on 30 January 1943, a last message arrived from Hitler. He was promoting Paulus to field marshal. Since there was a tradition in the army that 'a German field marshal never surrenders', the message was clear. 'He put the pistol in Paulus's hand', one observer said; in other words, Hitler had given him no honourable course other than suicide.

But for once Paulus ignored orders. Next day, he sent a message to Rokossovsky's headquarters: an offer of surrender for himself and his remaining ninety-six thousand troops. It was not a decision a man of his bearing could make lightly. He knew that the career he had so studiously built was now over and that he would be condemned as a traitor. He could also foresee that this defeat could lead to the crumbling of the grand offensive of which he had been a major planner, and that this could in turn lead to the downfall of the Third Reich, in which he had believed so ardently. Yet his act would at least bring an end to the carnage: Stalingrad had become the bloodiest battle in history, with well over a million lives lost on both sides.

When the emissary returned with Rokossovsky's acceptance, Paulus emerged from his subterranean headquarters in a devastated department store basement. He allowed himself to be loaded into a Soviet staff car and driven through the shattered streets to a wooden farmhouse in the suburb of Beketovka. There he was ushered into the presence of General Mikhail Shumilov, commander of the Soviet Sixty-fourth Army, acting for Rokossovsky. Shumilov, following protocol, asked for identification, and Paulus ceremoniously handed over his paybook. True to form, he stood erect, heels together, throughout the humbling ceremony. He was haggard, thin and unshaven, but he was wearing his last freshly pressed dress uniform.

TURNING HIS COAT

Hitler understood his fellow non-aristocrat well. Informed of the surrender, he predicted, 'He'll be brought to Moscow. There he will sign anything. He'll make confessions, proclamations … It won't be a week before he is talking over the radio'. In captivity, Paulus indeed joined the antiwar movement, and later Paulus testified for the prosecution in the Nuremberg war-crimes trials. Released from prison in 1953, he became an inspector of police. He was condemned for both his toadying to Hitler and for his last-minute conversion to anti-Nazism. He never again saw Coco, who might have said, 'I told you so'.

'Nuts!' Said the General

The Battle of the Bulge

It was 11 pm on 17 December 1944, when Brigadier General Anthony McAuliffe received the call. Outside, winter was closing in and the pines in the Ardennes Forest bowed low with snow. McAuliffe and the men of the U.S. 101st Airborne Division were retooling in Mourmelon-le-Grand, France, near the cathedral city of Reims. They needed to reorganise and to train replacements after suffering heavy casualties as a result of Operation Market Garden. The 101st 'Screaming Eagles' didn't expect to return to the front lines until mid-January at the earliest. Even the division commander, Major General Maxwell Taylor, had flown back to Washington for consultations and to spend time with his family. McAuliffe, the division's artillery commander, had taken over in his absence. Many of the unit's 11,500 men were Christmas shopping in Paris. The stay-at-homes were reading Christmas mail and looking forward to a promised Christmas dinner, lubricated with plenty of Reims's famous champagne. The feast was to be followed by a 'Champagne Bowl' football game between teams from the 506th and 502nd Parachute Infantry Regiments.

But one phone call changed all that. After he hung up, McAuliffe called his staff together for a midnight meeting. He didn't know where they where going in this snowy and generally miserable weather, he said. 'All I know of the situation is that there has been a breakthrough and we have to get up there.' Trucks were already transporting soldiers from the rear areas, along with their weapons and munitions, medical supplies, fuel and equipment.

German prisoners being rounded up following the collapse of Hitler's Ardennes offensive

So, at dawn on 18 December, McAuliffe, a West Pointer and career officer, hopped into a jeep and headed for Bastogne, a sleepy Ardennes market town at a crossroads near the Luxembourg border. At 9 am, the men of the 101st piled into trucks to follow him. That Christmas season, Bastogne would be the scene of an epic winter struggle, where a single defiant word from McAuliffe would be etched into the history books.

HITLER ON THE OFFENSIVE

Winston Churchill called it 'the Battle of the Bulge' because of the way German lines bulged into Allied-held territory. Eisenhower preferred 'the Ardennes Offensive'. To Adolf Hitler, it was first Die Wacht am Rhein, 'The Watch on the Rhine', and subsequently 'Autumn Mist', a masterstroke he had been concocting for several months. On 16 September, with the Allies eating up territory towards the German border, he had held a gloomy high-command meeting. Still disabled and with severe hand tremors following an attempt on his life on 20 July by a group of disaffected army officers led by Claus von Stauffenberg, Hitler sat unusually silent and motionless until someone mentioned the Ardennes, the invasion route through which German tanks had smashed into Belgium and France in May 1940. His ears pricked up. 'I have made a momentous decision!' he suddenly cried. 'I am taking the offensive!' He began to sketch out a plan in which panzer units would spearhead a drive through the forest, catching the Allies off guard and continuing on to the North Sea. The advance would split the Allied armies in two and capture the major Belgian port of Antwerp, vital to the Allies for supplying their vast armies.

Hitler's assembled generals looked at each other in amazement. Field Marshal Gerd von Rundstedt thought the idea was sheer lunacy. Field Marshal Walter Model said, 'This damned thing doesn't have a leg to stand on.' But Hitler would not be budged.

> The 106th Division was comprised mostly of eighteen-year old draftees fresh from college campuses; most had never fired a shot nor had one fired at them.

He ordered his chief of staff, Colonel General Alfred Jodl, to begin preparations. Jodl dutifully came up with a plan, revised it several times, scheduled the operation and postponed it. Then, as the snowflakes began to fall on the Ardennes, the date was set for 5.30 am on 16 December.

FEELING SECURE ON THE GHOST FRONT

The Allied-held side of the Ardennes was so quiet it was nicknamed 'The Ghost Front'. Part training camp and part rest facility, it stretched for one hundred kilometres, thinly manned by four divisions. The 106th Division was comprised mostly of eighteen-year-old draftees fresh from college campuses; most had never fired a shot nor had one fired at them. The Twenty-eighth Keystone was a veteran division but had been badly cut up in the Hurtgen Forest the month before and was now dominated by green replacement troops. The Allied high command, perhaps not having studied the history books, considered the Ardennes, with its razorback ridges, deep valleys, rushing streams and thick timber, a natural barrier to invasion, especially by tanks. For more than a week prior to 16 December, Allied intelligence detected the clanking and rumbling of equipment moving into place on the German side, but, feeling safe, the Allies paid little attention.

At the appointed hour on 16 December, the Ghost Front erupted. A massive cannonade blasted the American position for two hours. The Germans had amassed two armies of twenty-four divisions, led by seven armoured divisions totalling 970 tanks, plus nine hundred guns. Many German troops were green, too—by this time manpower-starved Germany was conscripting sixteen- to sixty-year-olds, with a few fourteen- and fifteen-year-olds thrown in. Still, these novices far outnumbered America's understrength and undertrained divisions.

Outrun and outflanked, the 106th collapsed. More than eight thousand men were quickly taken prisoner, among them Lieutenant Alan Jones Jr., the son of the division's commanding general. The Ninety-ninth Division also broke up in disarray, with half of its men becoming casualties or prisoners in the first few hours, one of its regimental commanders included. The Twenty-eighth Division was cut in half. Men streamed to the rear, throwing away rifles, equipment, overcoats; they were too inexperienced to know how to dig foxholes and defensive entrenchments.

In what seemed like no time, the Germans had advanced fifty kilometres, pushing the Allied line back into a wide pocket—in military terms, a salient—that became known as the 'Bulge'. A gloating Hitler thought he had Antwerp in his sights.

AIRBORNE TO THE RESCUE

More men were needed to hold the line. The nearest and most seasoned troops were the 82nd Airborne and McAuliffe's 101st. 'Hold Bastogne': that was the terse standing order given to McAuliffe by Major General Troy Middleton, commanding general of the XVIII Corps, after a breakneck race across France early on

A BRIDGE NEAR ENOUGH

As the Allied armies advanced into a collapsing Germany, one major obstacle stood in their path: the Rhine River. The Germans blew up or destroyed all the bridges spanning the waterway—or almost all. Unaccountably, they missed one. At 3.15 pm on 7 March 1945, troops of the Ninth Armored reached the river town of Remagen, between Bonn and Koblenz, and were astonished to find the Ludendorff railway bridge still standing. One platoon raced across the bridge, learned from prisoners that the span was to be detonated at 4 pm, and defused the explosives. Within ten minutes, 100 men had crossed the bridge and within twenty-four hours, 8000 men plus tanks were on the east bank of the Rhine. Five days later, four divisions had crossed the river and were headed towards Germany's major cities, Berlin and V-E Day.

19 December. He was echoed later that day by Major General James Gavin, acting commander of the Airborne Corps and McAuliffe's direct superior. Bastogne was critical to both sides. An otherwise unprepossessing town of four thousand people, it was the hub of seven converging roads leading into France. In the tortured terrain of the Ardennes, tanks could not manoeuvre as readily as they did in open country, so controlling these roads was vital.

As McAuliffe began organising the 101st for Bastogne's defence, Middleton gave him a vote of confidence. He told the commanding generals of the miscellaneous broken divisions and units around the embattled town that the defence of Bastogne was McAuliffe's show, and he would have final 'say'. 'He wears the star', Middleton said, referring to McAuliffe's brigadier-general rank.

The task McAuliffe was assuming was hardly promising. His most powerful antagonist was what the troops called 'Hitler's weather'. The skies over Bastogne were leaden, snow and wind lashed the armies. The German onslaught had overrun the garrison's storage depot, and the 101st was running short of ammunition, food and medical supplies. Yet airdropping was impossible in the hostile weather: four thousand Allied planes sat on the ground, unable to carry supplies or provide air cover.

... the 106th collapsed. More than 8000 men were quickly taken prisoner, among them Lieutenant Alan Jones Jr., the son of the division's commanding general.

A BLUNT COMMUNICATION

Later that morning, German General Heinrich von Lüttwitz's panzers snapped shut the ring it had been tightening around Bastogne. The town was now isolated, and cut off from reinforcement or resupply by road. In Washington, the 101st's commanding general, Maxwell Taylor, arrived for a Pentagon conference to be told, 'General, your division has just been surrounded', then went directly to the airport to return to Europe. At Bastogne, however, the news only raised morale. 'They've just surrounded us', said

Lieutenant Colonel Harry Kinnard, the divisional operations officer, adding cockily, 'The poor bastards.'

Kinnard's confidence stemmed from the knowledge that help was probably on its way. Supreme Commander Eisenhower, who had recognised early on that Hitler's attack on the Bulge represented a major offensive, not a mere local counterstrike, had ordered General George S. Patton's massive Third Army, then pushing east, to wheel his army ninety degrees towards the north and head to the relief of Bastogne. To redirect such a huge force was a monumental and complex task, comparable to turning an ocean liner, but under Patton's lash, by the morning of 22 December, the crack Fourth Armored Division was on its way, backed up by three full infantry divisions.

On the same morning, as McAuliffe was leaving his headquarters to inspect the battlefront, four uniformed Germans carrying a white flag arrived at the command post of the 327th Glider Infantry. Major Helmut Henke of the Panzer Lehr Division declared in halting English, 'We want to talk to your commanding general'. He displayed a letter in German and English addressed to 'the American commander'. The Germans were blindfolded and taken to McAuliffe's headquarters.

The Germans had ceased firing. A staff officer, Colonel Norman Moore, read the letter. 'What does it say, Ned?' McAuliffe asked. 'They want you to surrender', the officer said, going on to read that the Americans would be given two hours to capitulate before fire resumed and the Americans would face 'total annihilation'.

'Aw, nuts!' an irritated McAuliffe responded. He took the letter from Moore, scanned the English version and sat down, trying to frame his refusal. 'I don't know what to tell them', he told the staff.

Brigadier General
Anthony McAuliffe

'That first crack you made would be hard to beat, General', Colonel Kinnard said.

'What was that?'

'You said, "Nuts!"' Kinnard replied.

Grinning, McAuliffe asked for a sheet of paper and wrote, 'To the German Commander: Nuts! A.C. McAuliffe, American Commander'. (There are those who claim McAuliffe initially said something much earthier.) He handed the message to Colonel Joseph Harper and said, 'See that this is delivered'. The German officers were again blindfolded, then Harper tucked the message into Henke's hand. 'What does "Nuts!" mean?' Henke asked, puzzled. 'Is it negative or affirmative?' 'It is definitely not affirmative', Harper replied. Then, as the Germans planned to leave again under their white flag, he told Henke, 'In plain English, it is the same as "Go to Hell!"'

> ... McAuliffe asked for a sheet of paper and wrote, 'To the German Commander: Nuts! A.C. McAuliffe, American Commander'.

ONE MORE SHOPPING DAY TILL CHRISTMAS

Within the hour, German shelling resumed, and the encircling troops stepped up their squeeze. Baron von Lüttwitz felt confident that Bastogne would run out of food and fuel by Christmas and be forced to give up. But McAuliffe's tart and scornful reply quickly circulated through the U.S. troops, providing an enormous boost to morale. It even reached Patton, riding to the rescue like the old cavalryman he was. He radioed McAuliffe: 'Xmas Eve present coming. Hold on'. The 101st signals officer radioed back on 24 December, 'Only one more shopping day until Christmas'.

For a backstop, Patton went to church and in his own quirky way implored the Lord to provide good weather. 'Rain, snow, more rain, more snow—whose side are you on, anyway?' he prayed. 'I do not even insist upon a miracle. All I request is four days of clear weather. Amen.'

Whether or not it was divine intervention, by mid-afternoon skies were clearing and the waiting pilots were gunning their engines. Soon, while P-47s flew cover and bombed and strafed

German positions, transport planes began dropping supplies into a specially cleared area outside Bastogne. Within the next twenty-four hours, to the cheers of the besieged men, 241 aircraft dropped 214 tonnes of supplies, including K-rations, medicines, bandages—and Christmas mail. Meanwhile, the P-47s clocked up five thousand sorties blasting German positions and tank columns. One German officer said in awe that he could see a line of flaming vehicles all the way back to the German border. Alas, he said, they were German vehicles.

IMMINENT DELIVERANCE

On Christmas Eve, Tony McAuliffe, travelling by jeep, without lights but in bright moonlight, went to midnight mass in the tiny village of Savy. Mass was sung in a small chapel, in an abandoned seminary that had been converted into a hospital. While the 101st's wounded lay on the floor, some covered with parachutes from the airdrops, soldiers sang 'Silent Night' and 'O Little Town of Bethlehem'. McAuliffe crossed himself and gave thanks for what he saw as imminent deliverance.

At dusk on 26 December, McAuliffe was notified that the Thirty-seventh Tank Battalion, commanded by Lieutenant Colonel Creighton Abrams (who would become U.S. chief of staff in another war many years later), was arriving at the American lines south of Bastogne. McAuliffe went out to greet them. Captain William Dwight climbed out of the first tank and went to the hilltop where McAuliffe was watching. 'How are you, General?' Dwight said, saluting. The man who had faced down the encircling enemy with a four-letter word returned the salute and said, 'Gee, I am mighty glad to see you'.

Picture Credits

Index

Military operations are indexed
under their names, not under
'Operations', e.g. Anvil (operation).

Published in 2010 by Pier 9, an imprint of Murdoch Books Pty Limited

Murdoch Books Australia
Pier 8/9
23 Hickson Road
Millers Point NSW 2000
Phone: +61 (0) 2 8220 2000
Fax: +61 (0) 2 8220 2558
www.murdochbooks.com.au

Murdoch Books UK Limited
Erico House, 6th Floor
93–99 Upper Richmond Road
Putney, London SW15 2TG
Phone: +44 (0) 20 8785 5995
Fax: +44 (0) 20 8785 5985
www.murdochbooks.co.uk

Publisher: Diana Hill
Editor: Scott Forbes
Designer: Jacqueline Richards
Picture researcher: Amanda McKittrick

National Library of Australia Cataloguing-in-Publication Data
Title: Windows on WWII : a collection of iconic events from the second global conflict
ISBN: 9781741968583 (pbk.)
Series: Moments in History
Notes: Includes index.
Subjects: World War, 1939–1945.
    World War, 1939–1945—Miscellanea.
Dewey Number: 940.53

A catalogue record for this book is available from the British Library.

PRINTED IN CHINA.